What people are saying about *A.R.T.ful Leadership*

"The best learning is delivered in engaging stories and clear, understandable concepts. Larry Nordhagen delivers on both counts in *A.R.T.ful Leadership*. Here is a book that is a great read and a powerful learning tool. Every leader, regardless of their level of experience will benefit from his model of creating greater connections with the people within their organizations, which in turn creates improved results. This combined with the A.R.T.ful Leadership coaching and consulting services truly is an opportunity to bring transformational change to you and your organizations."

—Michael Howe, CEO Howe Associates, Inc. (former CEO of Arby's and MinuteClinic)

"Larry has created an exceptionally valuable roadmap on how to be or become a highly effective leader. The three tenets of *A.R.T.ful Leadership* ring true for me with Trust being most significant in this time of financial pressure and global competition. We have all witnessed leaders in our organizations and lives who have abdicated Trust for the sake of self-promotion and corporate advancement. Without Trust, organizations evolve into siloed fiefdoms of poor performing units isolated from each other and failing to leverage the tremendous human resources that live within their walls. Trust is earned over time and must be cultivated, day in and day out. It starts with speaking and acting honestly and encouraging open dialog throughout the organization. I highly recommend *A.R.T.ful Leadership* both as a book and a guide to living a rewarding life, both personally and professionally."

—Jim 'Woody' Woodburn, MD, MS, Director & Chief Medical Officer, Applied Pathways

"For those of us who find ourselves as company leaders (at whatever level/size/maturity), we need to learn how to effect change, particularly when it comes to performance issues. The problem-solving process we follow usually involves stages that include Defining, Measuring, Planning, Assigning Accountability, Executing, Monitoring, and Adapting.

Typically there is only one class of challenge where we ignore this tried and trusted path—ourselves. So if Larry can persuade one more person to 'park the ego' and get to work (through *A.R.T.ful Leadership*), his efforts will have been of service.

And, from a pedantic Englishman, anyone who can make a verb out of a 3-letter acronym deserves a hearing!"

—Mike Hartley, CEO CatchBull Ltd

"This is an excellent book that captures the vital elements needed for a successful diversity and inclusion practice, and it illuminates the influential skills required to lead today's constantly changing business environment."

—Eric Watson, Vice President, Diversity & Inclusion, Delhaize America

"A.R.T. ful Leadership, what a book! Excellent, brilliant, a must for any organization to add to their library; to implement if they want to run a successful organization. Keep it Simple; and YES by implementing *A.R.T.ful Leadership* within your organization you will be running an outstanding successful company. I LOVE the Four Key Steps and the Reflection Journal."

—Norma Heeley, Founder, Norcom Group—Asia Pacific

"Have you ever wondered how certain leaders "magically" have individuals following them across initiatives, companies, industries, geographies? The individual doesn't even care what role he/she will be performing, but just wants to be led by that leader. Why? Because she knows that no matter what, the leader has the ability to get the best out of her and cares enough to make her grow in any role or situation.

Now, have you ever wondered if *you* could be that leader? That "magic" is skillfully described in this unique book that wrestles with the intangibles of leadership—things we instinctively look for in a leader but cannot always articulate or distinguish—Admiration, Trust, and Respect. Like a good friend having a conversation with you, Larry, in his much loved casual, no nonsense style, systematically breaks down the components of a leadership style that has a lasting impact on the people being led. A unique gem of a book that whispers the age old secret of leading with a generous heart, creating sustained followership that 'pays it forward'"!

—Sarah M. Johansson, Vice President, United Health Group

"*A.R.T.ful Leadership* provides a deeply personal and relevant viewpoint on leadership. This book provides insight into not only *what* leaders need to do to be Admired, Respected, and Trusted, but *how* to get there. The examples will stop and make you consider your own leadership capability. As a leader, I am reminded what a wonderful, inspiring, and motivational experience it is to work at a company that truly 'lives' A.R.T.ful Leadership. It's ultimately the most rewarding experience—on both a personal and professional level—and something we should all aspire to in our careers."

—Stacy Hintermeister, VP, Account Director, Preston Kelly

"Larry Nordhagen delivers a path to building strong sustainable relationships. *A.R.T.ful Leadership* outlines a comprehensive model for anyone to leverage. I can not imagine success in my professional career and my personal life without people who I Admire, Respect, and Trust."

—Jon Dehne, Vice President Merchandising, Advance Auto Parts

"*A.R.T.ful Leadership* offers a perspective of leadership through the lens of the follower, truly making this a distinct difference then other leadership texts. In addition, the book provides a methodology and practical application techniques readers can immediately implement, no matter their level within an organization. Finally, the many scenarios included in the book add a real-world dimension that anyone will immediately identify with. A must read if you are serious about improving your leadership capability."

—Roger Olson, President, ODG

"Having worked in human resources for over 30 years I have worked with both A.R.T.ful Leaders and A.R.T.less leaders. I have worked with managers at all levels of an organization; I know both types of leaders have a profound impact on an organization, team dynamics, and the people they lead. My experience is that there are more A.R.T.less leaders in organizations, and human resource professionals can and should have a major impact on developing leaders to be A.R.T.ful (Admired, Respected, and Trusted). This book provides an excellent tool to help HR professionals achieve that end through thoughtful discussions and specific actions."

—Julie Buske, Vice President, Human Resources

"As a health care professional, a former colleague, and having been a student of Mr. Nordhagen's training courses over a few years, I can honestly say that he is a person I A.R.T. His years of leadership coaching experience along with his dedicated research have culminated into an effective leadership system. The pragmatic and logical approach of the A.R.T.ful Leadership model can be employed by any health care professional to enhance and improve their leadership skills."

—Anne Norman, DNP, FNP-BC

A.R.T.ful Leadership

The Path to be Admired, Respected,
and Trusted as a Leader

Larry R. Nordhagen

Pinnacle Performance Publishing
Minneapolis, Minnesota

A.R.T.ful LEADERSHIP

The Path to be Admired, Respected, and Trusted as a Leader

Published by: Pinnacle Performance Publishing, Division of Pinnacle Performance Systems Inc., Minneapolis, MN

Publishing consultant: Huff Publishing Associates, LLC

Cover and book design: Marti Naughton, sMart desigN

ISBN 978-0-9854911-0-9

Library of Congress Cataloging-in-Publication Data (to come)

Manufactured in U.S.A.

16 15 14 13 12 1 2 3 4 5 6 7 8 9 10

DEDICATION

To my children,
Alexander Frederick Nordhagen
and
Kathryn Mathea Lily Nordhagen.
Each day they challenge me to be
A.R.T.ful in my relationship with them.
They are my constant inspiration.
Thank you for being part of my life.

CONTENTS

FOREWORD

I met Larry in 1997 when we both worked for the same business, The St. Paul Companies (now The Travelers Indemnity Company). Back then we were often shushed for laughing loudly at some ridiculous thing one or the other of us did or said as we worked our separate projects. Over the years we kept in touch and have found ways to work together again and again—sometimes as contractor/client and sometimes internal to an organization. One of the reasons I continue to value my relationship with Larry is that he is honest (sometimes brutally so) about his own foibles, is willing to give me the same honest, reflective feedback, and (maybe most importantly) able to help me laugh at myself.

I watched, encouraged, and gave feedback as Larry began to develop the A.R.T.ful Leadership Model. We talked through various aspects, and he worked out the kinks with clients and employer groups. I was lucky enough to be working with Larry at MinuteClinic as the model really started to come together. The part that has been so exciting and inspirational to me is how Larry worked so closely with the leadership of that small entrepreneurial organization to develop and nurture an intentional and healthy corporate culture.

That is also where I saw how this model could so easily be applied to any other organization and how the fundamental aspects align well with my philosophy and my values. Treat people the way you would like to be treated, respect what each person brings to the table, and focus on making your team successful rather than on bolstering your own reputation.

No matter how you define success—and believe me, I define it differently than many people—this model works. Paying attention to how others view your actions means that the ends don't justify the means. Being an A.R.T.ful Leader means that there are no "little people" who "don't count" and who have to be manipulated by fear and intimidation. It also means we have to be mature enough to give and receive feedback in ways that build up rather than tear down the other person; to be in dialog with people that may not always agree with us, a skill that has fallen on tough times in our current public climate.

In this book Larry articulates for us in the 21st century what authentic, healthy, servant leadership can look like *and* provides the tactical steps for getting there. I believe strongly that this method could very well change your whole world.

Becky Swanson

ACKNOWLEDGEMENTS

I am indebted to the individuals who contributed greatly to the completion of not only the book but also to the A.R.T.ful Leadership Model and concepts that appear in the book.

First, I would like to thank Becky Swanson for her continuous support, encouragement, and time. Becky has been so inspired by the A.R.T.ful Leadership concept that she joined me in the effort to consult and coach others to become A.R.T.ful Leaders. Her contribution to the final product cannot be understated. Becky's continued thought leadership throughout the process is greatly appreciated. In addition, Becky was the first person to read the draft of the book and make recommendations for improving the text. I will be forever grateful to her contribution.

Next, I want to thank my wife Nancy. She has provided quiet encouragement and support throughout the process. She also did a fair amount of editing in the early drafts of the manuscript. Nancy understood my passion around A.R.T.ful Leadership from the initial concept to the research and formulation of the model and ultimately pulling it all together in writing the book. She also knew the timing was right to return to Pinnacle Performance Systems and dedicate my efforts full-time to A.R.T.ful Leadership. I am grateful to have had Nancy in my life for many years, and many more to come.

Many thanks to my editor Scott Tunseth. His thoughtfulness in editing the book cannot be overstated. His work was impeccable and his insight extraordinary. Scott brought things to the surface that I hadn't considered that added clarity and depth to the final product. Thanks Scott.

Michael Howe also has contributed greatly to A.R.T.ful Leadership. Michael was a strong supporter of the concept during his tenure as CEO of MinuteClinic. Since that time Michael has tracked my progress in writing the book. He has also provided me with suggestions along the way that added greatly to the final product. Michael also was kind enough to read the manuscript before being released. And finally, he allowed me to use him as an example in the book (although I didn't give him much of a choice).

To the other leaders who read the manuscript before it went to print, thank you for your time, your attention, and for your encouragement. The following leaders are individuals I Admire, Respect and Trust. To have them participate is tremendously gratifying: Jim "Woody" Woodburn, Sarah M. Johansson, Stacy Hintermeister, Ann Norman, Mike Hartley, Norma Heely, Roger Olson, Eric Watson, Julie Buske, and Jon Dehne.

I would like to thank the many individuals who took the time to complete the A.R.T.ful Leadership surveys. Your responses provided the data that was needed to identify the A.R.T.ful Leadership Drivers and Attributes. It is your experiences as leaders and your experiences with leaders that helped define what it takes for leaders to be Admired, Respected, and Trusted. Thank you.

Finally, to the many, many organizational members who have shared and will share their stories of A.R.T.ful and A.R.T.less leaders with me, thank you. You provide me with rich examples that bring A.R.T.ful Leadership to life. Your firsthand accounts bring relevancy to the A.R.T.ful Leadership concepts. Keep sharing!

PREFACE

Above my office desk, right above my computer screen, hangs a picture with three large letters:

A.
R.
T.

It has hung above my desk for years as a constant reminder to try and live an A.R.T.ful life. It is also there to remind me to get back on track when I slip. I hung it above my desk shortly after beginning to use the A.R.T. acronym in my work with leaders and discovering how the only way to become an A.R.T.ful leader and to sustain A.R.T.ful leadership is through constant attention to the principles.

The pressures we encounter in business, life, and with challenging relationships, A.R.T.ful leadership is not an easy task. But with constant focus and daily reminders, it can be accomplished. What I have come to realize is how rewarding A.R.T.ful leadership is personally as a leader and how meaningful leading A.R.T.fully is for those that I lead and influence. I also recognize the tremendous benefits that A.R.T.ful leadership brings to an organization.

The A.R.T. Leadership origin

A.R.T.ful Leadership was born during the time that I was doing a significant amount of consulting work at the Best Buy Corporation. During that time leaders continuously asked me the following questions:

> *"Why don't my people do what I ask them to do?"*
> *"Why don't my people listen to my feedback?"*

When asked these questions, I would ask the following questions in return:

"Why do the people that report to you not listen to your direction?
"Why do the people that report to you resist or reject your feedback?
"When your team does not receive feedback, what is missing that
causes them to reject your feedback?"

After some discussion, we would conclude that, fundamentally, individuals resisted taking direction and resisted feedback because the leader lacked credibility. The question then became, "why"?

I suggested the following: *Individuals are influenced by people they Admire, Respect, and Trust (A.R.T.).*

For a leader to influence effectively they must be perceived as Admired, Respected, and Trusted leaders. If individuals are not following direction nor listening to feedback, leaders need to ask themselves the following question: "What do I need to do differently to be perceived as an A.R.T.ful Leader?" The answer to this question will point to the changes that leaders need to make to truly be viewed as a credible leader. Leadership in the final analysis is about how you are perceived by those you lead.

I therefore created the foundational components for leaders to be effective at leading and influencing others. To create and sustain true followership required a leader to be:

A–dmired,
R–espected, and
T–rusted.

To make this relevant to leaders I have them answer the following: "Who do you go to for advice?" And, "Why do you go to this person for advice?" The answer always is that individual whom they Admire, Respect, and Trust. Further, no matter what advice they receive from that person, they will listen to it and will take action. The same holds true for leaders. Leaders must be Admired, Respected, and Trusted to truly be effective, to ensure that their directives are carried out, their plans are fulfilled, and their feedback is received.

When a leader is not Admired, Respected, and Trusted, feedback will be ignored, because it will have no value to the individual. As a leader you must work towards being perceived as someone who is Admired, Respected, and Trusted.

The A.R.T.ful Leadership concept began to resonate with people in leadership sessions and in conversations. From that point it was clear that A.R.T.ful Leadership needed to be a primary focus of my work. I then began a journey to answer the following questions:

- How can I clearly define A.R.T.ful Leadership?
- What distinguishes Admiration, Respect, and Trust?
- What are the drivers of an A.R.T.ful Leader?
- What do A.R.T.ful Leaders do to create synergy within an organization?
- What are the core competencies of an A.R.T.ful Leader?
- What steps would a leader who is serious about becoming an A.R.T.ful Leader take to be viewed as an A.R.T.ful Leader?

The goal of A.R.T.ful Leadership—the PATH to be Admired, Respected, and Trusted as a Leader—is to answer these questions. This book will provide you with an opportunity to learn about A.R.T.ful Leadership and provide you with an opportunity to explore your own A.R.T.ful Leadership path. Throughout the book you will be challenged to complete several Journal Activities. These activities will help you personalize your own journey to A.R.T.ful Leadership. Take this opportunity to grow as a leader. I have found this to be an excellent method for self-learning.

The stories in this book

The content of the book includes many stories. The stories are all true and have been selected to provide real examples that relate to the A.R.T.ful Leadership Model and concepts. The stories have been gathered through a variety of means. Some have been sent to me via email, some have been shared with me in personal conversation, others have been detailed in various surveys relating to A.R.T.ful Leadership, and finally, some I have observed firsthand. The vast majority of the stories contained in the book have been written to maintain the anonymity of all involved (the leader, the individual telling the story, and the company). When names are used, they are fictional in order to assist in storytelling. Names are not important (except in rare occasions). What is important in the stories is how they relate to the A.R.T.ful Leadership where they appear.

I have taken editorial freedom in the telling of most of the stories in order to increase the readability of the stories, and in some cases to add interest and perhaps a bit of humor. I want to be clear that all the stories contained in the book are real, and the facts contained in the stories are all accurate.

There are a handful of stories that do identify the company and the leader by name. When this is the case it met the following criteria:

1. It is my story and my example.
2. It is a positive example of A.R.T.ful Leadership.
3. I have gained approval from the individual to use their name and story.

I was sitting with an executive several months ago discussing the writing of the book. She wanted to know: "I have read many leadership books. What makes yours different?" This was an excellent question. What does make A.R.T.ful Leadership different? I replied that what sets this book apart from other leadership books is that A.R.T.ful Leadership centers on what a leader needs to do to be admired, respected, and trusted as a leader—nothing more, nothing less. The A.R.T.ful Leadership Model was created by looking at A.R.T.ful leadership from the perspective of individuals who have been led by A.R.T.ful and A.R.T.less leaders. The book is full of examples that provide powerful proof of the impact that leading A.R.T.fully or A.R.T.lessly has on individuals.

The journey to A.R.T.ful Leadership is relevant not only for providing leadership lessons but also for providing life lessons as well. Therefore, the journey to A.R.T.ful Leadership has the potential to be deeply personal and powerful for the reader.

To the reader

I am making the assumption that if you are reading this book you are either a leader who is intentional in becoming a more effective leader or a leader in training who wants to learn how to be an effective leader before you have to unlearn bad behaviors (a great idea). Therefore, I am writing this book to you as a leader. A "leader" is anyone who has responsibility to lead a business, function, or team. So as you read and see the word "you" I am referring to you as a "leader." I have chosen to do this in order to personalize the content and in so doing, hopefully make it more relevant to you, the leader. Finally, the terms "organizational members," "team members," and "individuals" are used to refer to people who either directly report to a leader or to those over whom a leader has some level of influence. These terms are used interchangeably to add to the readability of the text.

After hearing my response to her question, the executive I mentioned above said this: "That is different. I don't believe I have seen that approach before. I look forward to reading it."

I hope you are looking forward to reading this book as well. Enjoy the journey to A.R.T.ful Leadership.

"The Essence of A.R.T.ful Leadership"

Before you begin reading the book, complete the following Journal Activity to set the stage for your own journey to A.R.T.ful Leadership.

1. Access the following link and watch the 2-minute video:
   http://www.art-fulleadership.com/what-is-art/

2. Answer the following questions:
   - What are your reactions to the video?
   - Were you able to answer the questions?
   - Which ones couldn't you answer, and why?
   - What would it mean to you, your team, or you organization if you were able to answer the questions with confidence?

You will repeat this activity at the end of the book. Doing so will be one measure of your success in applying the principles of A.R.T.ful Leadership and demonstrating the A.R.T.ful Leadership Model.

Note: A compendium workbook is available that provides resources, worksheets, and tools to assist you in completing the A.R.T.ful Leadership Journal Activities. Visit www.art-fulleadership.com for details.

An Introduction to A.R.T.ful Leadership

A true test of a leader is not what they say about themselves but what others say about them.

Larry R. Nordhagen, *A.R.T.ful Leadership Point of View*, 2011

A.R.T.ful Leadership Defined

Before explaining the A.R.T.ful Leadership model, it is important to establish the definitions of the three components of A.R.T.ful Leadership. The definitions are similar to those you would find in many dictionaries. The difference is that the A.R.T.ful Leadership definitions of Admire, Respect, and Trust frame the A.R.T.ful Leader in leadership context. In addition, the definitions delineate the three components of the A.R.T.ful Leadership Model from one another in order to begin to distinguish the three elements. This delineation is important since each act independently and have identifiable "drivers" that influence whether you will be perceived as an A.R.T.ful Leader in any or all of the A.R.T.ful Leadership elements.

A.R.T.ful LEADERSHIP MODEL

A.R.T.ful Leadership: To be perceived as Admired, Respected, and Trusted in order to create true followership and sustain commitment by those you lead and influence inside and outside the organization.

A.R.T.less Leadership: To be perceived a leader who is not Admired, Respected, or Trusted by those they lead or influence. As a result, individuals lack engagement, commitment, and view the leader as ineffective.

Admire: To have a high opinion of a leader by virtue of what a leader is able to deliver to the organization, function, and team. Leaders who are admired are looked up to by those they lead due to the ability of the leader to act with integrity and connect to individuals.

Respect: To feel genuine appreciation and gratitude towards a leader. Individuals appreciate the leader for the mutual respect the leader shows to others and the energy the leader provides to ensure individuals and the team are successful.

Trust: The ability of a leader to build trusting relationships with those they lead. This is initiated by extending trust to others. Trust increases through building and maintaining relationships.

A.R.T.ful Leadership: The Big Questions

A.R.T.ful Leadership was born from leaders continuously struggling with the following questions:

> *Why don't my people listen to my direction?*
> *Why don't my people listen to my feedback?*

These questions have been asked and discussed in leader sessions and during one-on-one coaching sessions countless times during the time I have been working with leaders the past 20 years. These questions are also at the root of much management and leadership training (although not explicitly) on how to provide skills to leaders to ensure that employees are directed appropriately and are given feedback that they need to succeed.

It seems these two questions are always of concern to leaders. No matter what work that I have been asked to facilitate it seems that these two questions always come up in some form or another. Many times leaders tell me that they have applied all the rules they have been taught, and have perfected the techniques they have been introduced to during training sessions or by reading leadership books, and yet they still struggle with these questions. At times their struggle is with certain "difficult" individuals [their words]; with others, it is bigger struggle.

Much of the attention during my conversations with leaders was focused on "employees," meaning that leaders tended to focus the issue as a problem with the employees not doing something (taking direction and receiving feedback), instead of focusing on exploring the "why" behind the question. The "why" behind the question, or the question behind the question, would reveal the root cause for the individuals not following direction or listening to feedback.

It became clear after much dialogue with leaders and employees that the "why" clearly landed primarily on the shoulders of leaders and not with the individuals that they lead and influence (or in this case, struggle to influence). In some cases, leaders were not practicing proper techniques for providing clear direction or delivering feedback appropriately (although they think they are). In other cases, regardless of the soundness of the leader's technique, **how the leader was *perceived* was the barrier.** This fundamental truth was the answer to the "why" and became the core of A.R.T.ful Leadership.

Once it was clear that the answer to these questions resides with leaders, I asked leaders the following question:

> *"What could be standing in the way of your people following your direction or receiving your feedback?"*

As leaders struggled to answer this (because after all, if they could answer it they wouldn't have asked the initial questions in the first place) their frustration often increased. I suggested that leaders should perhaps consider a different approach in tackling this challenge and asked them this question:

"Could what is standing in the way be the result of how you are viewed as a leader? And if so, what could you do differently to gain credibility so that individuals would follow direction and listen to your feedback?"

In a receptive audience this will tend to put the *focus on the leader* and begin to change the conversation completely. In a non-receptive audience, I would quickly look at my watch and say, "Oh my goodness. Look at the time; I have a flight to catch." . . . and run for the door!

Leadership, or the lack there-of, stops and starts with self-leadership. *To be an effective leader you must first understand how those you lead and influence perceive your leadership capability.* How you are *perceived* by others will determine how you are *received* as a leader.

A.R.T.ful Leadership Foundational Questions

A.R.T.ful Leadership begins with leaders answering two foundational questions:

Who do you A.R.T.?
Who do you Admire, Respect, and Trust as a leader?
And
Who A.R.T.s me?
Who Admires, Respects, and Trusts me as a leader?

Who do you A.R.T.?

Why begin with this question? It is essential in becoming an A.R.T.ful Leader to begin by answering this question as accurately and honestly as you can. By answering this question you uncover the true alliances that you have as a leader both inside and outside the organization. The individuals that you A.R.T. are the individuals that you can consistently depend on for support. You can depend on those individuals on a daily basis without question. When you face challenges you can reach out to them and they will be there to sustain you, offering their assistance to overcome the challenges that every leader faces. The individuals you A.R.T. are critical to your success. It is important to know who they are, and to maintain your alliance with them.

When asked what characteristics organizational members looked for from individuals they A.R.T., those who answered the survey named these as the top five:[1]
- Support
- Advice
- Feedback
- Ideas
- A sounding board

Answering this first question will also clearly identify what limitations exist in a leader's A.R.T.ful network. When reviewing the list, a leader must consider if names are missing that should be on the list for the leader to truly be successful. If so, then the leader needs to determine how to move forward to expand their A.R.T.ful network. That is why this is the first question that leaders are tasked to answer in becoming an A.R.T.ful Leader and is closely linked to the second foundational A.R.T.ful Leadership question.

Who A.R.T.s me?

The answer to this question cuts to the heart of how you are perceived as a leader by those you lead and influence. Accurately answering this question is the determining factor in whether you as a leader *clearly understand who you are able to lead and influence* and *who you are currently not able to effectively lead and influence*.

Understanding this is a critical step in becoming an A.R.T.ful Leader.

Leaders often struggle in answering this question and, when answering, often struggle to look in the mirror and honestly assess why they are not perceived as A.R.T.ful by some. If you as a leader do not commit to understanding "why" individuals do not perceive you as A.R.T.ful, then you will likely not ever positively change those perceptions.

If leaders don't explore this question, they tend only to rely on the people that they already A.R.T., and this simply is not enough to be an A.R.T.ful Leader. Both questions are required to accurately determine not only what you perceive (Who do I A.R.T.?), but how you are perceived (Who A.R.T.s me?).

Remember the questions that were the impetus of A.R.T.ful Leadership?

"Why don't people follow my direction?
"Why don't my people listen to my feedback?"

Think about these two questions in your own life. When you resisted a direction you were given, what was the cause? When you didn't listen to someone's feedback or rejected someone's advice, what was the reason? Based on the research I have done over the years, I am certain that you (and countless others) resist direction and do not listen to feedback because you fundamentally do not Admire, Respect, and/or Trust the person delivering the message, and therefore the message lacks credibility for you.

If that is true for you, how effective do you think you will be in effectively leading and influencing the individual who does not Admire, Respect, and/or Trust you? The answer is not likely at all. And chances are, those individuals will over time become perceived as performance problems to you. In actuality it is how you are being perceived as a credible leader that is the barrier rather than the person's performance. (I know, you now have stopped reading and think I am a lunatic. Again, I urge you to think about your own experiences with an A.R.T.less Leader from your past in order to open your mind to this thought process).

Perceiving others as performance problems often leads to a contentious relationship between you as the leader and the perceived poor performer, and then you really have an A.R.T.less Leadership situation on your hands. Now you are going to start punishing the individual for not perceiving you as an A.R.T.ful Leader—which will certainly help the perception they have of you, right? And guess what: I have seen this happen over and over again in organizations. Employees have told me countless stories (some are in this book), and leaders have actually admitted this error to me (without necessarily recognizing it as an error at first). I am not saying that performance management process is never justified, so please don't make that leap. That is not what I am advocating, so let's cross that off the list of excuses for not being open to an A.R.T.ful Leadership approach.

When an individual does not A.R.T. you and you provide them feedback (it doesn't matter if the feedback is positive or negative), do you think it will be received? If you don't A.R.T. someone, your tendency is to reject the feedback, isn't it? It is natural to do so. So it would be reasonable to conclude that if the people you lead and influence do not A.R.T. you, your direction and feedback will not be welcomed or received either. That is the point. As the old adage says, "What is good for the goose is good for the gander." In other words, don't be surprised when those who report to you respond in the same way that you have responded to leaders you haven't perceived as being A.R.T.ful.

So the answer to the "Who A.R.T.s me" question is core to understanding how effective you will be as a leader. If the answer is "unknown" or "not positive," the action to take is not to pull back from those individuals, which leaders often do. Instead, be daring and ask yourself the question: "Who *doesn't* A.R.T. me?" The individuals that appear on this list need your attention. You need to take intentional actions to change their perception of you. This is what you need to do to attain A.R.T.ful Leadership.

A.R.T.less Leaders, on the other hand, make their "hit" list and begin a ruthless agenda to get the people on that list out of the organization, even though they may be top performers. This is much easier than having to look in the mirror, after all, and taking responsibly for the situation, right? Wrong. Remarkably, such action merely further degenerates the perception of the leader.

To recap, A.R.T.ful Leadership begins by tasking leaders to answer these two questions:

> *Who do you A.R.T.? Who do you Admire, Respect,*
> *and Trust as a leader?*
> *Who A.R.T.s me? Who Admires, Respects, and Trusts*
> *you as a leader?*

Typically, I have found in working with leaders that the lists of answers to these questions are shorter than they should be. The challenge then is to begin working on expanding both lists. The "Who do you A.R.T.?" list tends to be shorter than the "Who A.R.T.s me?" list. I believe this has something to do with people not trusting people and only allowing a few people "in."

What I have noticed over the years is that individuals tend to be able to recall A.R.T.less leadership examples more readily than A.R.T.ful Leadership examples. And sadly, many are not able to provide an A.R.T.ful Leadership example when asked the following question: *"Describe in detail a leader that you most Admire, Respect, and Trust inside an organization. What did the leader specifically do that gained your Admiration, Respect, and Trust?"* When allowed to provide an example in their personal life, they can complete the assignment, but often only after opening up beyond an organizational example. We are exploring some theories about why this may be true. These include the following:

- A lack of organizational commitment to employees in many organizations going back decades has a negative impact on A.R.T.ful Leadership.
- Employees are much more transient then in past decades. Leaders, therefore, have a shorter window in which to make an A.R.T.ful Leadership impression on those they lead. It can be done, but if a leader is not intentional about A.R.T.ful Leadership, a positive perception is unlikely. In turn, this exacerbates the transient nature of the workforce and the cycle continues.
- Organizations that only measure leaders for their financial results will likely not produce A.R.T.ful Leaders.

- Organizational policies and structures (at times) can preclude leaders from being perceived as A.R.T.ful Leaders.
- A lack of job security makes employees suspect of leaders, which makes it more difficult for leaders to be perceived as A.R.T.ful.

Once you have answered both foundational questions honestly, the next task is to determine whether the two lists are comparative, and if not, what actions need to be taken in order to gain some equilibrium between the two lists. To be an effective leader, "Who do you A.R.T.?" and "Who A.R.T.s me?" should be comparative. When the lists are comparative, a leader will be more able to lead and influence others, create excitement and energy within the organization, function, and beyond. That is the path to A.R.T.ful Leadership.

A.R.T.ful Leadership Research

Several methods have been used to define the A.R.T.ful Leadership Model and to identify the characteristics that lead to someone being Admired, Respected, and Trusted as a leader. The methods used included:

Field Research: Through the years field research has been conducted by watching leaders interact in a variety of situations, both within leadership groups and within their intact teams. These have included observations in a variety of organizations and industries. Field research provides direct access to leaders and individuals who they are responsible for leading and influencing. Observing these interactions and having the ability to make observational analysis and to speak with individuals concerning intent and actual impressions have been exceedingly helpful in advancing A.R.T.ful Leadership.

Interviews: Interviews have been conducted with employees (leaders to front-line employees) concerning the A.R.T.ful Leadership attributes. Interviews have ranged from formal to informal in nature. Informal interviews have resulted in recording field notes at the conclusion of the interviews (or conversations) in order to capture relevant data. In many cases, impromptu interviews have resulted in the richest data and have contributed to the collection of examples that have been used to identify specific A.R.T.ful Leadership behaviors.

Collecting Session Data: During a variety of leadership development sessions, participants have been asked to describe what behaviors or attributes have to be present in order for them to Admire, Respect, and

Trust a leader. The answers from participants have been compiled, analyzed, and crossed-referenced.

Surveys: Surveys have been administered to identify key A.R.T.ful Leadership attributes. The most recent survey was administered by inviting 350 individuals at all organizational levels from a variety of industries and age ranges.

Stories of A.R.T.ful and A.R.T.less Leadership: We ask individuals to record clear and specific examples (stories) of a leader demonstrating behaviors that result in a leader being Admired, Respected, and/or Trusted. We also ask individuals to record A.R.T.less leadership stories in which leaders have demonstrated behaviors that have diminished Admiration, ruined Respect, and/or destroyed Trust. These stories contributed greatly to identifying A.R.T.ful Leadership attributes.

The results of these methods have been combined to define the **A.R.T.ful Leadership Model** and to develop the **A.R.T.ful LeaderView 360** feedback process.

Research Continues

Continued focus surrounds gathering more examples, adding context to the model, and gathering data on the overall health of A.R.T.ful Leadership in organizations. There continues to be an effort to collect stories of A.R.T.ful Leadership in action. Stories are a powerful tool to make the connection between theory and changed behavior. When we conduct A.R.T.ful Leadership Coaching, we require leaders to keep an A.R.T.ful Leadership Journal. During each conversation we review the journal to discuss insights and lessons the leaders have observed in themselves and in other leaders. This is a powerful method for advancing A.R.T.ful Leadership capability. Keeping your own A.R.T.ful Leadership Journal as you read the book will be a powerful tool to your own growth. Continuing your growth by participating in coaching, training, or by simply reading our A.R.T.ful Leadership Blog Posts can also keep you growing as an A.R.T.ful Leader. These can be found at www.artfulleadership.com.

The Goal of A.R.T.ful Leadership

The goal of A.R.T.ful Leadership is to create true and sustained followership and commitment by those you lead and influence.

A.R.T.ful Leadership is not easy to achieve. A.R.T.ful Leadership is an intentional act and all three components are required.

The Key Drivers of A.R.T.ful Leadership

Through our research we have identified the following sixteen key drivers of A.R.T.ful Leadership. The Drivers are the essential characteristics needed for a leader to be Admired, Respected, and Trusted. The drivers will be introduced in this chapter, but each driver will be explored in detail in later chapters.

DRIVERS OF A.R.T.ful LEADERSHIP

ADMIRE

Deliver Consistent Results

Competent

Social Dexterity

Authentic

Represents with Credibility

RESPECT

Supportive

Demonstrate Mutual Respect

Responsible and Accountable

Provides Feedback and Counsel

Fair and Balanced

TRUST

Extends Trust

Keeps Confidences

Honest

Builds Relationships

Collaborative

SKILLED COMMUNICATOR

Admiration Drivers

The following are the five key drivers for a leader to be Admired by those they lead and influence:

Deliver Consistent Results: An admired leader delivers consistent results to the organization. This requires *devising a sound strategy* and *executing* on that strategy with and through others *flawlessly.*

Competent: An admired leader is well-versed in the industry and possesses a deep business knowledge. Has the ability to demonstrate leadership capability (in leading people). Demonstrates a tenacious drive to succeed and to motivate others to succeed.

Social Dexterity: An admired leader is adept at connecting with people and building a wide network both at an organizational level and at a social level. At ease in a variety of situations and contexts. Perceived as someone who can engage others in conversation.

Authentic: An admired leader demonstrates empathy and has a clear moral compass. Is self-assured and able to show vulnerability. Makes an effort to connect with individuals on an interpersonal level and cultivate interpersonal relationships.

Represents with Credibility: An admired leader is able to represent the organization, function, and team with the utmost credibility. Builds this impression with constituents both inside and outside the organization.

"I don't know everyone's name."
My Own Story of Admiration

The leader I most admired is Michael Howe, the former CEO of MinuteClinic, an organization that was on the verge of beginning a national expansion to reinvent healthcare delivery in America when I was asked to join the company to lead the learning organization. During the expansion, MinuteClinic grew from 30 clinics in two states to over 500 clinics across the U.S. in under two years. We were adding staff at the rate of 30% a month, which was quite an undertaking in itself.

I was responsible for all learning: clinical, leadership, managerial, operational. In addition, it was Michael's vision to create a strong corporate culture (more about that later); and to gain Joint Commission Accreditation.

When I joined the organization I was employee 25; when I left the organization three years later we had an employee population of over 1, 000.

Each Monday, Michael would gather the corporate staff and provide an update on how the organization was faring in the market and how the expansion was progressing. During these meetings he never used a slide deck or a script. Instead the meeting was highly conversational and informative. The meetings were well-structured but not to the point of being robotic like so many meetings that I have suffered through over the years. In fact, this was the only organization that I have been in where employees actually looked forward to the meetings. Michael had a unique ability to connect with every employee attending and everyone on the corporate staff was invited. Each week Michael would genuinely welcome new team members; somehow he knew who they were.

Another thing that I came to expect from Michael was for him to drop by my office at least once a week without notice. These visits were not to check up on me but were rather to inquire about how things were going and to offer support. These visits always included a conversation on a personal level. I always knew he was coming because I could hear him interacting with my staff before he would arrive at my office. He never missed an opportunity to engage with staff.

On one of these visits he seemed more reserved then his typical upbeat self. I took the opportunity to mention this to him. It may seem odd that someone would mention to a company's CEO that he didn't seem as upbeat as usual, but that is who Michael is and revealed the type of relationship and connection he had established with me. So, it wasn't odd for me to mention this at all. How he responded elevated my already high admiration I had for him.

Michael explained that he was a bit down because he had been walking around the office and realized he didn't know the names of a few of the staff. This was extremely upsetting to him. He told me that he had always prided himself in knowing each member of the staff at corporate and in the field by name. He had given up keeping up with the field staff several months ago because of the rapid expansion, but made a point to know the names of all the corporate employees. But now he realized that corporate had become too big too fast for him to remember everyone's names.

I was amazed that he even took the time or prided himself on such a detail as knowing the names of people. Particularly as the CEO. What CEO would ever make this a goal? Actually, I was shocked. For one, my own staff had grown so fast that I had a hard time remembering the names of those I interacted with infrequently. And here was the CEO who knew the names of every staff member at corporate until recently.

He went on to say that he now had to adjust and figure out how to stay connected to people in a different way, since the organization had grown to a critical mass. He was most concerned about keeping the "personal touch" that was core to the culture that had been established and was a real success criteria in our recruiting efforts.

For a CEO to hold each employee in such high regard was remarkable to me. I also recognized why Michael was admired by so many within the organization. It was the respect that Michael showed to others that lead to the mutual respect he received in turn. To me that was a teachable moment, which I have tried to emulate in my own leadership journey. Showing others respect through deep and genuine interest is a remarkable characteristic.

Respect Drivers

The following are the five key drivers for a leader to be Respected by those they lead and influence:

Supportive: A respected leader consistently demonstrates loyalty to team members and stakeholders. Provides assistance, information, and encouragement as needed for the function to be successful.

Demonstrate Mutual Respect: A respected leader demonstrates mutual respect by being approachable by all levels within an organization. Shows genuine interest in what everyone, regardless of level within the organization, has to offer and contribute to the organization.

Responsible and Accountable: A respected leader sets clear performance expectations and hold him/herself and others accountable.

Provide Feedback and Counsel: A respected leader is adept at providing feedback on a continuous basis. Promotes a feedback culture and views feedback as a necessary component for success. Asks for feedback as well as provides feedback.

Balanced, Consistent and Fair: A respected leader provides opportunities, rewards, and recognition to all members of the organization and team. Diligently treats individuals fairly and consistently (avoiding being perceived as having organizational favorites when rewarding, recognizing, or promoting individuals).

"Tells it like it is and watching my back"
A Personal Story of Respect

The leader that I Respected was my manager for over seven years in three different organizations. I have deep respect for her leadership abilities, which is why I followed her to two different organizations over five years. Julie Buske first became my leader many years ago while I was with St. Paul Companies (now The Travelers). When she moved to Adaytum (now Cognos) she recruited me to lead the learning organization. Again, years later she convinced me to suspend my consulting practice and join MinuteClinic.

As I thought about why I specifically respect Julie as a leader, I had to step back and think about it, because the respect that I have for her definitely grew over time. I followed her to different organizations for the opportunities that the positions provided to my career, but just as important to me was the opportunity to be part of her leadership team. So here are the specific reasons why I respect Julie as a leader:

First, she earned it. It isn't easy for me to let people in. By nature I am a cautious individual. Particularly when it comes to people in leadership positions (sorry, I just am). I have had too many experiences with leaders who did not show respect for people who were not at the same level.

I believe Julie sensed that I was cautious of her, so she treaded lightly at first. She adjusted her leadership style to meet me where I was at the time. She recognized that I was a high performer and leveraged my skills, including my ability to lead people. I was always consistently recognized for my achievements; she never took credit for my work. She knew that when I looked good, she looked good; this seemed easy for her because she clearly was confident in her own ability. I have found that some leaders find accomplishment of their people a threat to them. She didn't.

Second, Julie let me lead. From the start she let me lead my area of the function without interruption. She gave me complete autonomy. She acted as an advisor and didn't try to control what I did or take leadership away from me. She knew how to leverage resources appropriately and maximize talent—and that included me.

Third, Julie offered support when needed. When I needed her to remove barriers or step in to assist she was always willing to do so. She would first make sure that it would be the right thing to do, and if I really did need her to step in, she did without hesitating.

Fourth, Julie was always willing to listen whenever I needed a sounding board to bounce ideas around or to discuss various strategies that I was considering. There never was a time when she made the decision for me. She always made herself available for these discussions. Her door was always open—always.

Fifth, when I needed a "wake up call" Julie would provide me with feedback. Actually, the feedback was expected and I often asked her for

14

feedback. It was natural. When I needed feedback, she would provide it in a manner that never felt as though she was being critical or that she was reprimanding me. She approached feedback in a way that I knew she was providing me with information that I needed to be more effective. If she ever heard something concerning me she would bring it to my attention immediately. The best part was that feedback was a conversation. I am grateful that feedback was instilled in me as something that was an everyday part of interaction with her.

Those are the reasons that I have a deep and lasting respect for Julie. It is also the reason that although we are no longer in the same organization, we remain close and I consider her a friend. Julie is someone I A.R.T., and I know she A.R.T.s me. It is reciprocal.

Trust Drivers

The following are the five key drivers for a leader to be Trusted by those they lead and influence:

TRUST

Extending Trust: A trusted leader must extend trust and lead with trust. Demonstrating trust fosters trust in return.

Keeps Confidences: A trusted leader must demonstrate a high level of integrity in maintaining confidentiality. Individuals must know that when they provide information to a leader in confidence that the leader will keep that promise. If that promise is broken, information sharing will stop.

Honest: A trusted leader must demonstrate a high level of openness in discussions with those they lead and influence. This requires a leader to be straight forward in providing information that is critical to assist individuals to do their jobs or be successful. Information needs to be timely and needs to be delivered in the right medium to be appreciated.

Collaborative: A trusted leader is able to share leadership in order to bring the best ideas and solutions to the forefront. This is also evident when a leader works tirelessly to create networks and partnerships both inside and outside the organization. When leaders are able to create and sustain strong connections and resource bonds they increase the perception of being a trusted advisor to those they lead and influence.

Relationship Builder: A trusted leader has the ability to connect with individuals at a personal level that leads to open communications and strong bonds/commitment. Building strong relationships aids in positively motivating and encouraging others.

"I Don't Know Who Else I Can Trust . . ."
A Story of Trust

I was having a horrible time with my manager. No matter what I did we clashed. If I said the sky was blue, she said it was orange. If I said "yes," she would say "no," If I said "up" she would say "down." You get the picture. I loved my job, but at the time I hated my leader. I tried everything I could think of to get in her good graces but nothing worked. I tried to avoid her, but that only worked part of the time. I couldn't avoid her completely. Thank goodness, I worked remotely.

The main issue that we had was the bi-weekly meetings that I had to come into the office to attend. It seemed those were the occasions that we would butt heads the most. To attend the meetings, I had to take a half day to travel to the office and back to my home office again, taking me out of contact with my customers. Quite honestly I didn't find the meetings very fruitful and merely put me way behind with work when I returned to my home office. Even so, I tried to make the best of it, knowing that I had difficulty with my manager.

I made sure I was on time for each meeting, so as not to upset her. I certainly didn't need one more thing for my manager to be on my case about. However, there was never a meeting that started on time because my manager was perpetually late. And I mean not just one meeting, and not just a little late. She was way late—anywhere from 20 minutes to a half-hour. As I waited I would reach out to make sure the meeting was still on. I began to do this because sometimes I would wait around just to find out that something had come up and the meeting had been cancelled. I would also reach out to see when the meeting would start so I could perhaps touch base with a couple of my customers while I waited in order to stay productive. When I would do this, it really sent her over the edge. If she responded at all it was very terse. And when she would show up she would be critical and quite nasty. So every two weeks I would be subject to her calling me out for every little thing she could think of that had happened the previous two weeks. I couldn't figure it out, because quite frankly everything was going very well. I was at my wits end. I was a long-time professional, had a long track record of being successful, and have never been treated so unprofessionally. Clearly I was being punished for simply asking a question regarding the start time of the meeting.

This continued to the point that I considered leaving the company, even though as I said before, I loved my job and the people I interacted with as part of my responsibilities. I reached a point where I just couldn't do it much longer. I had to talk to someone, but who? Trust is a big issue for me, and it was not a core competency in the company—another issue for me I must say. I certainly didn't dare speak to my manager's manager, since I knew they had worked together at a prior organization. I figured that would not do me well. I thought about HR for about half a minute, but I didn't even know who to call in HR. Then it came to me . . .

I had the opportunity to work with a leader from another division within the company on a project a short time ago and I thought of him. "John" seemed to be a straight shooter, and in all of our meetings and conversations he seemed to be level-headed, up front, and reasonable. He always provided sound advice so I took a risk and sent him an email that said, "Need advice on a delicate issue that requires the highest level of confidentiality. Are you up for it?" The response I received was, "Yes. When would be a good time to chat? Should be over the telephone, not on email." I was immediately relieved that I had taken the risk and couldn't wait to talk to John, if for no other reason than to just have someone that would listen.

When I spoke to John he assured me that our conversation would be kept confidential. He also told me he was humbled that I had reached out to him for advice and that he took this with great responsibility. This really put me at ease. I then opened up and explained the entire situation without holding anything back. He listened and only interrupted to get clarity on a couple of things. Then he offered advice on how to think of the situation from my manager's point of view. At first I was taken aback, but what John said made perfect sense. I had never thought about it from my manager's perspective before. I guess I was too close to the situation. John offered me suggestions for how I might handle the situation differently going forward. It completely opened by eyes to the situation and on how to manage my manager more effectively.

Since that time things have changed for the better. I no longer fear the bi-weekly meetings. The relationship with my manager is improving and I don't have the stress that I was experiencing before. I am so thankful that I could trust John to help me change things for the better.

Skilled Communicator Driver

The Skilled Communicator Driver cuts through all three elements of A.R.T.ful Leadership.

> **SKILLED COMMUNICATOR**

Skilled Communicator: This is a leader who communicates openly and honestly. A leader who is a skilled communicator delivers information with ease and confidence. Answers the "why" for individuals in order for people to understand the rationale for decisions that have been made by the leader and/or organization. Allows and takes part in open dialogues and exchanges and enjoys healthy debates on topics that are of concern to the organization and team.

The Relationship between Admiration, Respect and Trust

Is there a relationship between Admiration, Respect, and Trust? What impact does one of the elements of A.R.T.ful Leadership have on the other elements? Can a leader be Admired but not Respected or Trusted? I have asked and been asked these questions countless times by people over the years. Clearly there is a connection between the three A.R.T.ful Leadership elements. There are also some, but not many, relationships between some of the drivers within the model. The drivers have been carefully selected to remove redundancy in the model.

It is clear that the three elements—Admiration, Respect, and Trust—work independently. For example, if you think about the leaders that you have had or currently have, I am sure there are certain leaders that you Admire but may not Respect and/or Trust; and there are yet other leaders that you may Respect but that you do not Admire or Trust (and so forth). You get my point.

What I have gathered through my research is this: Admiration, Respect, and Trust operate independently. But, here is where it gets interesting. In most of the feedback we have received, it would seem that for a leaders to be **Trusted**, *they first* need to be **Admired** *and* **Respected**. Another way to put this is that **Trust is the most difficult of the three to earn** from people. So the A.R.T.ful Leadership Equation it would appear is this:

So as you read on, be prepared to make a commitment if you want to succeed as an A.R.T.ful Leader. I hope you do, because I know A.R.T.ful Leadership reaps rewards on several levels:

Organizational Rewards: As an A.R.T.ful Leader you will have the ability to influence and motivate with greater ease than ever before. You will find that your organization will have a renewed energy, drive, and excitement that didn't exist prior to leading A.R.T.fully. Organizational results will improve with the new energy, excitement, and focus that is a result of your A.R.T.ful Leadership.

Relational Rewards: Those who practice A.R.T.ful Leadership are rewarded at a personal level in many ways. It is my experience that A.R.T.ful Leaders often find that they are rewarded greatly in the deep relationships they form through living the model. Practicing A.R.T.ful Leadership will improve your relationships in every facet of your work and home life. I know this from personal experience as I have gained from the relevancy of practicing A.R.T.ful Leadership in my own life.

Personal Growth Rewards: Practicing A.R.T.ful Leadership provides an opportunity for personal growth and in many ways is an opportunity to self-actualize. You will see that A.R.T.ful Leadership very quickly becomes very personal. It isn't a model or journey where "one size fits all." Once you understand and learn the model, you will begin to flex the model to fit the unique daily challenges and opportunities that you face every day. As you open yourself up to be vulnerable about how you are perceived as a leader and take responsibility for those perceptions you will embark on a journey of self-discovery and personal mastery. Take this tremendous opportunity!

The rewards that A.R.T.ful Leadership has to offer make A.R.T.ful Leadership a unique way to look at and experience leadership. It is also why I have dedicated my professional life to this work. I am passionate about bringing A.R.T.ful Leadership to the attention of today's leaders and to offer it to the leaders of the future.

What do you want your leadership legacy to be? Do you want it to be one where you are remembered as a leader who merely held a leadership position? Or, would you like to be remembered as a leader who is Admired, Respected, and Trusted, and emulated by those you lead?

The choice is yours to make.

My Own Personal Journey to A.R.T.

(Losing It and Getting It Back)

My experience in both my personal life and professional life as a coach, friend, and mentor is this: how people respond to the defining moments in their lives determines whether they will view themselves as "victims" or "survivors." Our point of view will predetermine in many ways our attitude, our energy, our ability to persevere, and our ability to live a joyous life in many respects. Each one of us has defining moments, and those moments are opportunities to build character instead of being circumstances that knock us down. That is why when I coach leaders I look for opportunities to learn about their *defining moments.*

In order to put my own A.R.T.ful Journey into perspective, here are some of my defining moments:

- In 1981 I was driving a van in Montana. I came over a hill and was hit head on by a 16 year-old driver. I woke up and I was hanging upside down. It looked like I was looking out red curtains—it was my blood. I was trapped in the car for several hours. I was unrecognizable. Every bone in my face was broken except for my nose. My teeth were still in my mouth, but they just weren't attached to the roof of my mouth. If I would have passed out I would have drown in my own blood. My hip and leg were shattered. I was in the ICU for three weeks. It took six months to get to a point when I could walk again and twelve months to get teeth back in my mouth. The last surgery on my face was in 1999.

• The day my children were born. What great joy.

• 9/11/2001. I was the head of global learning and development for Adaytum Software. It was an incredible company making huge noise in the financial software space. We were moving from smaller sales to enterprise sales and a web solution. Much was changing and the company was taking big risks. That September morning we had a group of salespeople in the Twin Towers in NYC finalizing a deal with the New York Port Authority. The company was banking heavily on that sale going through, but of course it didn't. Adaytum was acquired by Cognos a short time later. I was laid off within two months and started Pinnacle Performance Systems consulting and A.R.T.ful Leadership shortly thereafter.

• **The** day that I received a certain phone call from my son Alex . . .

I was leading the learning organization at MinuteClinic during the time of rapid expansion. The A.R.T. concept was adopted by MinuteClinic as a foundational component to the MinuteClinic culture. The notion of all organizational members being A.R.T.ful was embedded in every component of learning. Practitioners who joined the organization were introduced to the methodology on the first day on the job. During that time I traveled extensively conducting culture sessions with leaders and new employees across the country.

During the sessions, I would challenge individuals to reflect on how to become more A.R.T.ful in their organizational lives and their personal lives. This exercise often leads to some deeply moving discussions. One evening while sitting in a nameless hotel in a city that I don't even remember, it dawned on me that I was in an A.R.T.ful Leadership crisis of my own. How could I possibly be driving others to lead A.R.T.ful lives when I was not doing it myself? It became clear that I had to correct my own path in order to be authentic about what I knew to be a powerful method to lead and influence others. It was time to take a long hard look in the mirror and take steps to be more A.R.T.ful in my own life.

So what had brought me to this revelation? My relationship with my son Alex. At the time my son had just turned eighteen and was a sophomore at a college where I was an adjunct faculty member. He had purchased a condo and was working full-time in addition to college. Yes, he is an overachiever. Since he had moved out on his own, the only times that I had a chance to see him were during brief times between classes on campus. I mentioned to my wife that I missed him being around and that I wished that he would come over to the house to visit or call more often. My wife said that he didn't because he was avoiding me. Avoiding me? But why would he be avoiding me? She then explained, in her not so subtle way, that I often criticized our son for everything he did. And now that he didn't live at home he could avoid my constant scrutiny by staying away. I immediately went into denial. The discussion continued—with me defending myself—explaining that I was hard on him, because I wanted the best for him and was merely trying to keep him from doing stupid things. I wasn't trying to hurt him; I was trying to help him. My wife didn't buy it. She attempted to get through to me that when our son shared information with me I responded negatively by finding something wrong with what he had done or finding something that could surely go wrong in a decision he had made. I wasn't ready to listen and passed it off as my son just being too busy with his newfound freedom to spend time with us. Still, the seed had been planted.

Although it was hard to accept, slowly over several days and weeks I kept thinking about what my wife had told me. I also started to replay conversations that I had had with my son in my head. What I came to realize was my wife was right. My intensions were pure, but my execution was contemptible. I needed to change how I interacted with my son if I was to be perceived as an A.R.T.ful father. I had been extremely critical of my son and would tend to point out things that were wrong with what he had done or things that could go wrong with the decisions he had made or was considering. Therefore he had started to shut down and share less. And yes, to avoid me.

I began to share this experience during A.R.T.ful Leadership sessions in order to show how A.R.T.ful Leadership starts with the individual, not anyone else. I also began to share how things began to change as I began to change and how I started to repair my relationship with my son.

The strategy: I had to begin to rebuild the relationship and to regain an A.R.T.ful relationship with my son.

I Needed a Strategy

Making a change in the situation with my son required a conscious effort. It required some clear strategies:

Strategy #1—Make the Call: One thing that my wife had said during our conversation kept running through my mind: "Do you ever call him, or do you always wait for him to call you? The phone works both ways you know." So I began to call my son and just check in. The conversations were short, just asking questions about how things were going with work, school, and how things were shaping up with some projects he was doing at his condo. Just quick small talk conversations to keep connected.

Strategy #2—Keep Advice to Yourself: I stopped giving advice when I spoke to my son. Even when I was screaming inside my head to say something, I kept quiet. I also used a tactic that I often teach leaders to use, which is: "When in doubt, ask a question." This phrase ran through my mind constantly when talking with my son and I used it often. This helped me to avoid criticizing him. Instead I would ask him questions that would potentially lead him to his own answers—always a much more self-empowering strategy.

Strategy #3—Let Him Know I Am There and I Care: The last strategy that I tried to utilize was to let him know that I was there to support him or help out as needed. And to offer this without any strings attached (as I previously tended to do). I would try to remember to end each conversation with, "Do you need anything?" I decided to begin to take a more proactive approach and offer my support instead of waiting for my son to ask.

The Result

Progress was slow, as it is when you have not previously demonstrated A.R.T.ful Leadership. And that takes me to another hotel room just outside New York City and the phone call. I will never forget the phone call. I was in my hotel room preparing for an A.R.T.ful Leadership session when my cell phone rang; it was my son. I didn't recall the last time it was that my son had been the one to call me, but it had been months. I answered the phone. As usual I kept the conversation light and then he said, "Dad, I need your advice on something." I can't express how significant that moment was for me. I couldn't remember the last time he had come to me for advice, and for good reason. So, this was the moment of truth. Would I blow the opportunity to do it right this time? Or would I take advantage of all the work I had done, and really show A.R.T.ful Leadership? Would I begin to be perceived with more Admiration, Respect, and Trust?

Instead of starting out of the gate with what I would do, I listened closely to what my son's issue was, what he had done about it to date, and what he was considering doing as a next step. I made sure this time that I knew the entire situation before pontificating. I asked questions, explored various scenarios, and worked through different consequences for each decision that he was considering. Then, and only then, did I suggest a couple of ideas that had not been explored. It was a good conversation. When the conversation ended and we hung up, I am not ashamed to say, I wept.

The next day I had a compelling story to tell how to put A.R.T.ful Leadership into action and a success story to share that is deeply personal. I had worked hard to regain my son's A.R.T.—and I was richer from putting in the effort. After that phone call, the calls began to be more frequent, and to this day I try to do everything I can to be perceived as A.R.T to my children, because they are my A.R.T.

This is why I so deeply believe that leaders must ask themselves the following questions repeatedly and answer them honestly:

> *Who do you A.R.T.?*
> And
> *Who A.R.T.s you?*

How am I doing with my son? This story is several years old now. Since that time my son has married and continues to do well. I couldn't be more proud of him. I still am a father who wants the best for his children and have high expectations that I have to fight to keep to myself at times. So I try to be A.R.T.ful in my interactions; some days I do better than others. I do my best to be A.R.T.ful more often than not and keep my eye on the ball so the phone keeps ringing.

A.R.T.ful Leadership Reflection Journal

1. What is your A.R.Tful story? When you have lost it and gotten it back?

The RAT

10 Flaws of A.R.T.less Leadership

It may seem strange that this book dedicates a whole chapter to A.R.T.less Leadership. I am doing so because it is important to distinguish A.R.T.ful Leaders from A.R.T.less leaders. The best way to do this is to begin by highlighting the top 10 mistakes leaders make that prevents them from being Admired, Respected, and Trusted. As you read, you can consider these 10 Leadership Don't's, or Flaws. In the final analysis, when these 10 Flaws are turned into the affirmative you will have 10 powerful means to help achieve A.R.T.ful Leadership.

This chapter title actually was the result of the following story that a leader shared with me. As I considered the title "The Rat," it dawned on me that when you changed the order of the letters of A.R.T. it spelled RAT, and that caught my attention. So, we begin the discussion of A.R.T.less leaders with "The Rat."

"The Rat"
A Story of the A.R.T.less Leader

Six months ago I survived an experience with a leader that was one of the most horrendous experiences that I have encountered. We nicknamed "Tami" "The Rat." Why "The Rat"? Because you couldn't trust her. You never knew when she might come for you next, so you never dared let your guard down. The Rat was seemingly the most wonderful leader imaginable. There was one critical character flaw most people failed to recognize: she was only in it for herself and to build an empire. She would promise you the world as long as you followed her lead and were completely devoted to her. She was a complete control freak. Anyone who crossed her was blacklisted. But if you were one of her puppets, you were on easy street.

I never trusted her; there was just something about her. She kept trying to convince me to have my department moved under her regime, but I wouldn't do it. She promised me promotions and larger control if I did. I wasn't interested.

The Rat started to make bigger and bigger moves to show just how marvelous she was to our parent company. We found out that she was making trips to the home office and was bad mouthing several of our leadership team in an effort to make herself look good. None of what we heard she said was true, but we knew she was positioning herself to gain more control and seize more power.

I was preparing to launch a new initiative that was to have a major impact on the business. The Rat was one of the main stakeholders of the program. I began to hear rumors that she had assigned the ownership of the program to one of her favorite leaders within her team. I wasn't told. She also began to meet secretly with my staff to design the program without my knowledge. When my staff came to me with this information, I invited myself to the meetings. When I did, she cancelled them. Something was definitely up. I tried to schedule a meeting with The Rat to discuss the issues, and she declined.

Eventually I received a phone call from one of The Rat's direct reports confirming that indeed something was up. The Rat had told her that she was close to getting my department under her leadership in a new organization structure that was underway. And, when announced, she was going to make moves to get me out of the company, since she couldn't control me.

I confirmed this with several other members within The Rat's organization. What The Rat didn't realize is that few trusted her and were more than willing to share information with me. With this information I was able to start making moves to keep myself and my staff safe.

I will be brief in saying that I was able to counter her attack and was able to keep my department from moving under her organization. But the toll it had on me and my team was significant. Many of us left, although on our terms and not on The Rat's terms.

What is remarkable is how one person can have such a profound negative impact on so many people inside an organization. After I left, I learned The Rat had been relieved of her duties.

"Rats" are a good metaphor to use for A.R.T.less leaders (with apologies to the rat lovers out there). After all, rats are widely feared and hated in the modern world. Rats are characterized in literature as being dirty, devious, cheating, lying, and mistrustful. In gangster movies of the 20's and 30's James Cagney coined the phrase, "You dirty rat," which indicated that someone was a lying despicable individual that couldn't be trusted (although Cagney was often playing the gangster). Finally, if someone "rats someone out," they go and tell someone something that they shouldn't, Rats, for the most part, are not represented well, poor things. As you read the "10 Flaws of A.R.T.less Leaders" you will see the link between the characteristics of A.R.T.less leaders and those of rats.

When I think of A.R.T.less leaders, and I know this will seem like a stretch to many (but the rat thing probably does as well), it always conjures an image of "The Goops." "The Goops" is a song that my mother-in-law would sing to my children at the dinner table when they were young and they were not demonstrating good table manners. The words are:

"The Goops, they lick their fingers. The Goops, they lick their knives. The Goops, they wipe their mouths on the tablecloth . . . They lead disgusting lives!"

Now you know what I mean by it being a stretch. But whenever I come across an A.R.T.less leader or am told about an A.R.T.less leader, I can't help but to think to myself, "What a Goop!"

Ten Flaws of A.R.T.less Leaders

A.R.T.less leaders impact organizations and team members negatively. The more of these flaws a leader demonstrates the greater the damage the leader causes within the organization. A.R.T.less leadership damages the team and lowers productivity in the following ways:

Low commitment/engagement: Team members have a diminished commitment to the organization.

Lack of cohesion: Team members lack cohesiveness and do not collaborate with one another. They may collaborate outside the team or with certain members within the team, but collaboration across the team will be highly unlikely. In fact, a team lead by an A.R.T.less leader will likely have a team that is made up of many cliques.

Lack of motivation: Team members will lack motivation. Energy is tapped by trying to navigate the A.R.T.less leader. This is a huge distraction.

A lack of commitment: All this leads to a lack of commitment and passion for the work and the organization. Team members will potentially stay with the organization and hope that they will outlast the A.R.T.less leader. If they can't take it anymore, and they are in the position to do so, they will seek a transfer. If all else fails, they will look for opportunities elsewhere to escape the leader.

A.R.T.less leaders exhibit 10 flaws that result in team and organizational dysfunction. Leaders who exhibit several of these behaviors will not create and sustain committed followership nor will they be able to positively influence others. They will be perceived as someone who is not admired, is not respected, and can't be trusted—A.R.T.less.

The 10 flaws of A.R.T.less leaders:
1. Micromanage
2. Do not share information
3. Do not engage with their team
4. Play favorites
5. Do not admit mistakes
6. Believe they are the smartest people in the room
7. Take credit for good results
8. Find scapegoats for poor results
9. Do not hold others (especially their favorites) accountable
10. Do not speak the truth and lack the ability to hear the truth

Flaw #1: Micromanage

A.R.T.less leaders who micromanage individuals within their organization are not able to influence organizational members in a positive way. In fact, micromanaging only serves to disengage employees and limit creativity. Micromanagers spend their time controlling every aspect of what people do and how they do it. Control is achieved by giving people directives and not allowing people to deviate from directives. Deviations are met with harsh consequences. A.R.T.less leaders believe that if they control every facet of the operations their expectations will be assured.

Leaders who micromanage don't trust their teams to take responsibility. This in turn breeds mistrust for their leadership within and across the team. Team members begin to distrust one another and begin to form cliques within the function. Alliances begin to form as survival instincts kick in; team members begin to identify who can help them figure out how to stay safe in a hostile environment.

Individuality is squelched by a leader controlling every aspect of their environment. People are afraid to step outside of the very specific boundaries that have been set by the leader. People stop taking initiative because it is easier to just do what they are told. Team members spend most of their time and energy making sure they don't do anything that may upset the leader.

The Corporate "Soup Nazi"[1]
The Story of "Peggy," an A.R.T.less Leader

The following story is one of my favorite A.R.T.less leadership examples. It is extremely funny in a sad way for the individuals who were subject to this leader. It demonstrates how resilient individuals become in the face of A.R.T.less leadership.

A few years ago I was an internal consultant in a large organization. Collectively our team possessed 100+ years of consulting experience. My team was part of a larger division that we could leverage as resources to support the solutions that we developed for our customers.

There was a growing tension between our consulting group and the resource group. Both groups reported into "Peggy" who was the senior leader of the division. We started to hear rumors from the support team that they had been told by Peggy not to support us. It was very odd. When we brought this to the attention of our manager, he was evasive. Clearly there was some truth in what we had heard because the support began to dwindle.

Over time the situation became progressively worse. Peggy removed administrative help and other support from our team. We ended up having to do everything on our own. We couldn't use the large support staff for anything. We were told if we wanted to continue to provide services we would have to seek support from our customers. This simply would not work.

From there Peggy started to keep our team from offering various solutions to the business. As she did, she reassigned these solutions to individuals who reported directly to her. Slowly she was beginning to cut us out of key initiatives that were a major part of our work. Again, when we tried to engage Peggy in discussions, she wouldn't have it.

Peggy's final move was to reorganize the division and replace our manager with an individual who was a complete "Bobble Head" for Peggy. The consulting group had no previous contact with our new manager except for all-division meetings. The announcement was made during a department meeting. In typical fashion an organization chart appeared on the screen. What was odd is that the organizational chart was represented as cylinders that looked like soup cans. The new structure made no sense except that Peggy had carefully placed the people who would simply ask no questions and wait for her to tell them what to do at the top of each stack of soup cans.

After the meeting the consulting group met secretly. I asked, "What's up with the soup cans?" and everyone laughed. I also said, "And what's up with the new leadership group? Peggy really has groupthink going on now doesn't she. She is like a Corporate Soup Nazi!" Everyone laughed hysterically and from then on, Peggy was known as "The Soup Nazi" or "SN" for short.

We agreed that we had no idea why we would be reporting to our new manager, but we feared it wouldn't be good, and we were right. In the first week we didn't meet with our new manager; she didn't even ask us to meet the first three weeks. SN began her reign of terror by peppering us with emails:

She took away major business owned programs that the consulting group ran and moved it to other soup cans—"No programs for YOU!"

She began to dictate what we could and could not do any longer, including providing solutions to the business—"No consulting for YOU!"

She stopped our group from partnering with business leaders to provide business direction recommendations—"No decisions for YOU!"

She required us to account for every minute we spent (which was reduced to moving paper)—"No professionalism for YOU!"

She started to blame our team for anything that went wrong—"No accountability for YOU!"

I can't describe how traumatic this time was; no one can unless they have lived through it. It is one of the most stressful times I have spent in a job. SN methodically destroyed a highly functional team of professionals. We spent all our time and energy focusing on survival and moving out of the organization. This Corporate Soup Nazi was insignificant to my future, but had such an impact on my work and home life at the time that is was ridiculous.

Thank goodness we were able to coin the SN nickname for her; it kept us sane much of the time. It brought great comic relief to my team for several months as each of us escaped that toxic environment and moved to better places.

Flaw #2: Do not share information

Information is power, isn't it? To A.R.T.less leaders it is, and that is why they keep it to themselves. When everyone in their organization has to beg for information to do what they need to get done, then they believe they are more powerful. Nothing could be further from the truth in a high-functioning and productive organization.

Withholding information merely slows down a highly productive team. It doesn't allow individuals to have what they need to be responsive to the market or to the customers they are responsible for serving.

This behavior applies not only to disseminating information, but to a leader excluding their team from access to information. A.R.T.less leaders will exclude individuals from meetings they should attend, with the result that team members are not provided information that is essential for them to be successful. Instead, not only will the leader continuously block the team from meetings, he or she will be the sole representative, and if is unable to attend, will not send a substitute.

So why do some A.R.T.less leaders do this? What is the motivation? In speaking to individuals who have been led by these leaders and in coaching leaders away from this behavior, here are what motivates these leaders:

The leader doesn't trust their team with the information. They are afraid what their team may do with the information if they share it, so they keep it to themselves.

The leader lacks confidence. Since they are not confident in their leadership ability, they use informational power as a means to validate their leadership role.

They believe they should be the in charge of editing any information provided to their organization or team. They do this by deciding who needs information within the team and when they need it. This mentality merely prevents information from being disseminated in a timely manner. As a result individuals begin to seek information outside of their own functional area and begin to use their networks and the grapevine to keep informed—not an ideal or productive culture.

"Block and Tackle"
The story of "Tim," an A.R.T.less Leader

My leader blocks me from everything that I need to do my job, and I am at my wit's end. I can't get him to provide me access to people or information.

"Tim" hired me to increase productivity. To do this I need to dig into what is currently happening to determine where improvements are needed. When I ask for reports or access to information, I am met with resistance. Before Tim lets me see anything he has to "check it" first to see if there is anything sensitive before I can have access to it.

I learned that only Tim has access to many of the files and that Tim doesn't allow anyone to have access to most of the information. When I inquire about information from people I am told, "You will have to ask Tim for that. Good luck; it won't happen." When I would receive information it looked like something you would get from the CIA; things would be deleted, or there would be parts missing.

Tim blocks me from participating in meetings or contacting key customers whom I need to speak with to uncover issues. Tim tells me that he would let me know if there was anything I needed to know. Trouble is, he doesn't know what I need to know because if he did, the company wouldn't be in the shape it is in.

When I discussed my frustration with a couple of people in the company they said that it is just the way it is, and if I want to keep my job I better get used to it. It didn't seem like anybody knows anything except for Tim.

I realized that the function really was comprised by a bunch of lackluster, unmotivated individuals. It is clear to me now that Tim is the problem. The unfortunate part is, Tim doesn't have a clue, and I don't think he wants to get a clue.

Flaw #3: Do not engage with their team

A.R.T.less leaders often do not connect with their team. And, if they do engage with their team, they do it either very awkwardly or inappropriately. A.R.T.less leaders who suffer from this flaw tend to know that they don't do this well, but instead of working on their social skills and working to make connections they just hide in their office. This simply alienates them further from their team, and therefore further diminishes the influence they have with their team.

When A.R.T.less leaders do engage, they tend to do it in writing via an email to avoid a dialogue. When in person the leader tends to make a presentation and, again, avoids a dialogue. When they do contrive a conversation, they talk and talk and talk about what they want to talk about or what they are interested in rather than what the group is interested in or would like to discuss. (What the team would like to discuss doesn't even cross this type of leader's mind.) Finally, this leader makes sure there is always an excuse not to join any team function. If there is a social or semi-social event for the function, this type of leader will make sure there is a business conflict. And if this type of leader does ever attend, working the room is not something that you will see the leader do.

The following story is an example of this flaw among leaders. The story presents an example of a leader being called out for inappropriate communication with another leader within an organization.

"Don't Roll Your Eyes at Me"
The Story of "Mari," the A.R.T.less Leader

A former collogue of mine has no interpersonal skills. I don't miss having to work with "Mari" for a minute. She is one of the most dislikeable individuals I have ever met. And this is hard to say, since I am a person who looks for the best in everyone. I couldn't find that in Mari.

Mari had a perpetual frown 24-7. She refused to make any effort in conversation, and even simple pleasantries were beyond her. The people who reported to her never seemed to last long with the organization, and, of course, Mari always said it was their fault.

I tried to work with her as little as possible, but there were times when I didn't have a choice. When I did have to interact with her I tried to be as charming as I could. It never seemed to work. Mari just simply seemed to hate her job, people, or life in general. She just could not be pleasant to save her life.

Once, after requesting information from her via email, I received the usual non-response, I very nicely reminded her after a couple of days that I needed information from her, and still nothing. After a week, I decided I was going to have to stop by her office and talk to her (ugh). When I stopped by her office and said, "Good morning. How are you?" she did not respond. I reminded her that I needed information from her for an upcoming meeting the next day. Mari looked up, scowled, grunted (I think it was a grunt, but it also sounded like right before I got to her office she had finished eating a rodent), and ROLLED HER EYES at me. That was my breaking point. My kids don't even do that, and they are under five. I said calmly and with disbelief, "Did you just roll you eyes at me?"

She was stunned. She sat up like she had been electrocuted. She said, "Whhhaat?" Bad question, Mary, because this allowed me to ask her again.

I said, "Did you just roll your eyes at me?"

She just stared at me. So I decided to use this as a "teachable moment." I said in the most conversational voice you can imagine, "I would appreciate it if you would not roll your eyes at me again. I have requested information and have been waiting for over a week. Inquiring on the status of that information simply requires an answer, not an attitude. Please provide me with the information by the end of day. Have a great day."

Mari's social skills didn't improve, but she never rolled her eyes at me again.

Flaw #4: Play favorites

An A.R.T.less leader who plays favorites will be sure to cause rifts in the teams they lead. When a leader distributes rewards disproportionately to only a few, the members who received the rewards are perceived as "favorites." This causes fractures and discord within a team. In addition, when a leader does not recognize all team members nor provide opportunities for promotion or opportunities to lead initiatives fairly across the team, this also causes deep and lasting resentment across the team. The have-nots view the leader as A.R.T.less, and the "haves" are resented.

Leaders showing favoritism are damaged, because the favoritism diminishes team cohesiveness, commitment, and overall team moral.

"Hello Friend"
The Story of "Phil," an A.R.T.less Leader

"Phil" is my executive leader. He plays favorites and isn't shy about it. A couple of the team members are great at playing up to Phil and have truly become his stars simply because they laugh at his jokes, fall all over him, and hang on his every word. Two of them have been rewarded by being promoted for their efforts with Phil. These two receive constant accolades in meetings and in emails expressing how great they are and how much they contribute to the division, while the rest of us are ignored. No matter what anyone else does, Phil somehow gives the credit only to these two.

The other day Phil was coming down the hallway towards me and stopped in front of one of his favorite's offices as I approached him in the hallway. I said hello to Phil. He barely acknowledged me and then he turned and loudly said to my peer, "Hi friend!"

Seriously? "Hi friend"? Did Phil really have to just say that in front of me? Did Phil just nearly ignore my existence and then verbally hug my peer? Did I just feel devalued? Yes. Did Phil want to send me a message that I was completely insignificant? Congratulations, Phil, on your leadership prowess.

Flaw #5: Do not admit mistakes

When leaders believe they need to be infallible to be perceived as leaders, then they will likely not admit a mistake. This leader will likely not step up to the plate to acknowledge a mistake and move on. This creates those uncomfortable "Elephant in the Room" moments that everyone has to ignore—at least until they are safely away from the leader's earshot. That's when the gloves come off and the "elephant" is talked about by team members.

Leaders need to understand that when they admit mistakes they are actually admitting their humanity. This actually is appreciated by those they lead. When leaders admit their mistakes they actually add to their credibility. When leaders don't admit to or recognize their mistakes or missteps, team confidence erodes.

"Elephant in the Room"
The Story of "Bill," an A.R.T.less Leader

My leader "Bill" thinks he is perfect and loves to point out everyone else's mistakes. Bill not only points them out but will harp on them in front of others; he loves an audience. He even likes to make fun of people.

When Bill makes a mistake and you point it out, however delicately, he simply refuses to take ownership. He will defend anything he does to his dying breath. Later, after the fact, he will make a correction but not ever admit that he has done so.

Bill drives me crazy, Bill drives everyone crazy. Bill lacks any credibility with his staff. It is nearly impossible to support him, because you can't have open and honest dialogues with him. On top of that I am always walking on eggshells around him because I know he can't wait to make me feel small. It must be nice to be perfect. I wouldn't know what that feels like, because Bill tells me I am not on a daily basis.

Flaw #6: Believe they are the smartest people in the room

This flaw is demonstrated by A.R.T.less leaders who have overinflated egos or who lack confidence and so are desperately trying to justify their leadership status by acting as though they are the smartest person in the room. Whatever the motivation, this flaw is devastating to a team.

Through the years I have encountered many leaders who have this complex, and I have spoken to many individuals who have been subjected to this flaw. Here are the following characteristics that the smartest people in the room tend to demonstrate:

Competitive: Fundamentally the smartest person in the room wants to win—at all costs. Winning means that their idea is the best, and no other idea should even be considered.

Argumentative: Since their ideas are the best, they will argue with anyone who attempts to challenge them.

Defensive: When challenged, the smartest person in the room will become defensive and attack the person who is challenging them. Being the smartest person in the room causes him or her to use harsh words and be extremely aggressive to stop any challenge.

Controlling: They never consider anyone else's ideas. This is accomplished by controlling conversations. They will talk and you will listen. They state what they want to happen and when it will happen and how it will happen. They don't ask for agreement; they demand agreement. Done!

The result of having a smartest person in the room as a leader is that the people they lead begin to be disenfranchised. Since team members don't seem to have any ability to impact what or how things will be done, they merely are pawns for the leader to manipulate. And when things go wrong, the leader will likely not step up and admit to having a bad idea. Instead, they will look for a scapegoat (another flaw), because, after all, they are the smartest person in the room.

"I am Always Right"
The Story of "Kent," an A.R.T.less Leader

Kent is the executive of my division. He has seven divisions that report into him. Sadly I am one of the people that leads one of the divisions. I am often baffled why Kent has anyone in leadership positions because he doesn't leverage us at all. He doesn't let us lead our respective divisions. You see, Kent is always right, and his ideas are always the best ideas. Actually he wouldn't know what his leadership team's ideas are because he doesn't care to listen to them. In our weekly meetings it is Kent time. He talks and we listen. If we attempt to answer his questions he stops us in our tracks. When any of us begin to make a suggestion about what we would like to do he shuts us down. Only Kent's ideas see the light of day.

There are a few members of the leadership team who have gone off on their own and done things against Kent's wishes. They hope he won't find out about them. However, when he does it isn't pretty. Kent makes a public display of their "radicalism" (he actually has used that word). One of the leadership team was fired for implementing something that was not approved by Kent. And we are the leaders in the company. Kent is so ineffective. It is a matter of time before Kent's castle begins to crumble, but I am sure it won't be his fault.

Flaw #7: Take credit for good results

An A.R.T.less leader is one who will always take credit for positive results while not recognizing team contributions. This leader instead takes the credit for the team's contributions and successes. A leader may do this to advance his or her own reputation or status in the organization (outside of the team).

When this A.R.T.less leader ignores the team's contributions, the lack of recognition the team receives causes a drop in motivation over time. They wonder why they are working so hard when the A.R.T.less leader continues to reap all the accolades for achievements of the team.

Leaders demonstrate this flaw primarily through the way they communicate. They turn the achievement of the team into a personal achievement by using "I" statements in acknowledgement rather than "we" or "you" statements. They simply don't refer credit to the team or to specific team members.

Here is an example of a Chairman offering a compliment to an A.R.T.less Leader who takes all the credit for team achievement:

Chairman: "Tom, your team did a great job on the Juniper project. It was a tremendous effort."

A.R.T.less Leader: "Thanks. It came out exactly as **I wanted it to. I** didn't know if the team could pull off what **my** vision was for the project, because it was pretty aggressive. But in the end I kept pushing them and **I did it**. Thanks so much. I really appreciate it. I will let the team know how much it means to you."

The A.R.T.less leader didn't attribute the success to the team, as called out by the Chairman, but instead took all the credit. Here is what the leader said after returning to the team, calling them together and sharing the information with the team:

A.R.T.less leader in an all-team meeting: "I had a conversation with the Chairman last night at a leadership function that I was asked to attend. He came up to me to tell me what a great job **I did** in executing the Juniper project. I wanted you to know how pleased he was. He couldn't be happier with the project. I told him that you all were able to pull off **my vision** and came through **for me** in the end."

Again, the message delivered to the team was clear: *I*, the leader, executed the project based on *my* vision. The team may have helped the leader pull it off, but they received no direct recognition for their efforts. The A.R.T.less leader communicated how good the team made the leader look, but not how well the team performed. This was not an accurate representation of what the Chairman actually expressed to the leader. The leader distorted the Chairman's gratitude for the team's performance.

"Narcissist"
The Story of "Craig," an A.R.T.less Leader

My leader "Craig" is very charismatic. I was excited to join the organization to have an opportunity to work with Craig. During the first month on the job Craig was open to me stopping in and discussing different projects that he wanted me to review. I noticed that my colleagues rarely talked to Craig, which I thought was odd. It should have been a warning sign, but I was too green. Craig also invited me to tag along to several client meetings to be introduced to several accounts that I would be assigned to in the coming months.

After the first month, access to Craig stopped. Craig emailed my assignments, although my office was literally about 15-feet from his office. When I had a question, Craig would cut me off and tell me he was too busy. Clearly it would be a "trial by fire." I began to struggle to learn the "system" with little to no communication or help from anyone. It seemed that Craig was finally beginning to act like everyone else in the office (or vice versa).

I began to learn the ropes pretty quickly when Craig told me that if I didn't pick it up, I would be gone. So much for "nice Craig." He told me that if I "didn't start making him look good, it wouldn't look good for me."

My colleagues didn't offer me any help, but a couple did provide me advice. They told me that it was all about making Craig money. The more money you make Craig the better it will be. Work nights, work weekends, and don't bill that time to the account. Working off the clock is how you get ahead. So I did. And, it worked. This formula worked really well for Craig. I won't get into the details, but in essence if I could complete in one month a project that would normally take three months, and do it by working 80 hours but only billing the account 40, then Craig would make more profit. I didn't, but Craig did.

As I played the game, Craig began to tell me "How good I made him look." I hadn't seen my family for months, but Craig was happy.

Craig would bless you with a bonus (which I could never figure exactly out how it was calculated). But when he would bring you in and tell you about it, it would make you feel dirty. He would tell you what a great job he did at bidding the project and how grateful you should be that he was on top of things and how lucky you were to work for him. Never once did Craig tell me what a great job I did. It was always about him—always.

I hated that job and feared Craig. When I was recruited by one of the top clients of the firm I left without ever speaking to Craig. The client I went to also stopped working with Craig's firm, since they pulled all the work in-house under my lead. When I left I never looked back, but I did learn what kind of leader I never wanted to be.

Flaw #8: Find scapegoats for poor results

This is actually the opposite of Flaw #7. This is a leader who looks for scapegoats for anything that may go wrong within the function they lead. An A.R.T.less leader will never take any responsibility or be accountable for lackluster results. Instead the leader will look for someone within their team to take the heat for them. Holding people accountable for their work is justified, but this is a leader who actually publically broadcasts faultfinding, and often unjustly.

But this flaw isn't really about a leader holding someone accountable. Holding people accountable is done privately between a leader and the individual. Finding a scapegoat on the other hand, is a leader passing the buck and publicly deflecting responsibility in order to protect the leader's status within the organization. The A.R.T.less leader therefore seeks a "sacrificial lamb" that is expendable.

The result of this flaw? For the scapegoat, of course, it's not good, and the team will be fearful that every time something goes wrong they may be next. Hopefully, at some point in the wider organization the A.R.T.less leader will be held accountable before too much damage can be done.

"I Couldn't Do Anything Right"
The Story of "John," an A.R.T.less Leader

I was new to the organization and was aligned with "John," a senior executive in the company. In my role, my job was to act as an internal resource to aid John to improve performance within the organization. The role suited me perfectly.

I have always been known as a person who can get things done and someone who achieves superior performance—always. Another attribute that I possess is the ability to create strong relationships with clients, employees, and superiors. So, I immediately began trying to build a relationship with John, since this has been a critical success factor for me throughout the years.

I had heard stories that the organization I had joined was not a "relationship" place, and word on the street is that the company has a culture that "eats you up and spits you out." However, I was sure I could be successful; I always had been in the past. I couldn't have been more wrong.

I met with John a couple of times a week, but I just couldn't seem to connect. It was like talking to a cold brick wall. He simply would not open up to any type of questioning or dialogue I attempted to start with him.

John was unwilling to engage, to provide information, to participate, or to actively partner. He was, however, more than willing to be hyper-critical. I tried to stay positive. I kept my energy level high and tried to remain upbeat. But this actually was met with contempt. John actually didn't like you to appear upbeat. The expectation was to act sullen. It was weird. It was like walking through mud. It was incredibly wearing, and I was using every trick in the book to keep motivated.

After three months, things were going as well as could be expected, at least with the work, if not with relationships. I was getting things done and moving initiatives forward. I thought it was time to sit down with John and ask for some feedback. My objective was to have John acknowledge all the work I had done to date and to consider objectively what next steps needed to be achieved. To trigger the conversation I prepared a document that provided a progress report of all the work that I had done since joining the organization (both completed and underway).

What I didn't expect (but in hindsight should not have been surprised) is what happened. Asking John for feedback was an opportunity for John to beat me up. John told me everything I had done wrong from day one (it had been three months, remember). Apparently I had really been bothering him. He didn't have any concrete examples, and when I tried to get specifics that seemed to just irritate him more; so I just listened.

When John was "spent," I asked him, "Well, what has gone well the past three months that we can build upon going forward?" He sat there for about three seconds and said, "I can't think of anything."

Wow. I have never had anyone at any time in my career provide such hurtful feedback. This after giving everything I have and having no one willing to partner or support me. Clearly I could have done things differently or better; everyone can. But "nothing"! No, that was not acceptable. I realized then what a cancerous organizational culture I had joined.

Shortly after that meeting I figured out why John was always critical of what I did. Here is what was happening: John was reviewing all my work after it was concluded with his boss, who was one of the most negative individuals I have ever met. Thus, being true to the culture. John's boss would never find anything she liked, so she would immediately criticize what had been done. John not wanting to take the heat for anything would immediately place the blame on me. Although John was in complete agreement with what we had done, the blame was placed entirely on my shoulders.

Once I figured out the game I tried to get access to John's boss to prevent this from happening, but John blocked me. So I learned to live with the constant criticism and learned to let it roll off my back for the short time I remained with the organization.

What I was able to do after the first and last feedback session with John was to choose my words carefully, watch my back always, avoid setting myself up to be blasted by John, and most importantly I never again asked for feedback.

Flaw #9 – Do not hold others (especially their favorites) accountable

A leader who lacks the ability to hold others accountable does so at the expense of team productivity. People who are not held accountable are left to their own devices to hold themselves and one another accountable. However, holding one another accountable is not likely to happen if accountability is lacking in the leader.

A lack of accountability within an organization begins to break down a team. Team members begin to feel resentment for the leader who is not stepping forward and holding team members accountable for lackluster performance. Leaders who ignore poor performance tend to lien more heavily on the strong performers, which, in turn, puts a strain on those individuals. As the strong performers begin to wear down they begin to resent fellow team members who are not producing the same results and are "skating by" without any consequences.

A.R.T.less leaders exhibiting this flaw will lose credibility to leverage resources appropriately. They are often viewed as being miserable at managing performance since they do not set performance expectations. Much of this stems from being conflict averse. They find it difficult to deal with individuals who are not performing. Until such leaders can move forward and change the way they approach performance and do it consistently, they will be perceived as A.R.T.less leaders.

"And He Can Have Wine for Dinner Because?"
The Story of "Gordon," an A.R.T.less Leader

I selected this story to represent this flaw because it shows the lack of a leader holding everyone on the team accountable using the same standards. As you read the story you will also notice it has flavors of Flaw #4—Play Favorites—as well.

Accountability only works for certain individuals in my group. That would be me and two of my peers, but not for our colleague Mike. He can do anything he wants.

There are four of us who are part of the implementation team. Three of us travel about 80% of the time. Mike, however, only travels about half of that. We have no idea why he doesn't have to travel as much as we do. When he is in the office he doesn't do anything but surf the web. He tells us he doesn't like to travel (join the club, pal). Apparently he has complained to Gordon, who gives the rest of us more of the workload and doesn't make Mike take on as much.

Last month our boss went on a tirade over our expense reports. He told us that we were spending over the per diem. None of us even knew what the per diem was. We were told we would not be reimbursed for more than $40.00 per day. And no alcohol could be expensed. We looked into the policy, and that isn't what it stated. It was a "guideline" but not a policy. But, no matter, that is what we had to do. (Ever tried to eat in NYC on $40.00 dollars a day?) . . . except for Mike, that is.

Several weeks after this I was talking to Mike and mentioned how hard it was to keep expenses at $40 a day. Mike said, "What do you mean?" I explained about Gordon coming down on us. Mike said he didn't know what I was talking about and that he never turned in expenses with meals less than $60 per day. How could you when you order wine with dinner (he actually said that). He said he never has an issue with his expense reports. I asked him some other questions and found out that he didn't have to follow any of the travel policies that the rest of us had to follow.

Needless to say, I shared this information with the rest of my peers. We don't believe a word Gordon says and don't want anything to do with Mike; they can have one another. We all have put in for transfers.

Flaw #10: Don't speak the truth and lack the ability to hear the truth

Leaders who are not willing to speak the truth to those they lead and keep information from their team will be viewed with suspicion. Leaders who do not have open channels of communication and who only communicate partial information when they do share information are not dependable sources for the team. The team will begin to utilize other sources to seek information and begin to develop informal networks to get information.

Closely associated with this flaw is the flaw of reacting badly when hearing the truth, particularly when the information is perceived as bad news. When leaders react badly to information, team members will begin to shut down and keep information to themselves. Even if the information is innocuous, the team will begin to stop information flow in fear of how the leader will react.

"Stop Yelling at Me"
The Story of "Beth," an A.R.T.less Leader

"Beth" is the VP of a call center. I report to Beth. She was a high-energy and committed leader. I respected her ability to keep on top of seemingly endless priorities without missing a beat. We met often to discuss day-to-day operations. She had great insight and was terrific at coaching me through operational issues and staffing problems. During those conversations she would provide suggestions that I could implement immediately. The problem occurred when Beth was faced with news she didn't like; when this happened she became unbearable. If everything was going well, Beth was great, but when things were challenging, Beth would become a monster.

Every two weeks I was required to report on the call center numbers. Often the numbers weren't perfect. This happened all the time, because the numbers that had been established were completely unrealistic.

I tried to get Beth to push for different goals to be established, but that didn't work. So every two weeks I would walk into her office with great trepidation. She knew the report would not be good, because it never was. She would turn to the last page of the report and begin to scream. I would try to interject, but she wouldn't listen and would keep on screaming what a bad job I was doing, what a bad job my team was doing, and on and on and on. Every two weeks.

I dreaded these meetings. I couldn't sleep the night before the meetings, and the stress was becoming unbearable. And then the day came when I couldn't take it anymore.

As usual, I handed her the report, she turned to the last page, and started in. I could feel myself begin to lose control. All of a sudden I leaned forward and I yelled, "STOP SCREAMING AT ME!" I don't know who was more surprised, me or her. It was followed by a very, very awkward silence. She sat back in her chair in shock.

I regained my composure and apologized, but I said I just couldn't take her yelling at me every time I brought in the report. I told her that screaming wasn't productive. I explained that I dreaded every meeting, and I simply couldn't go on.

Surprisingly, she apologized. From that day forward she didn't scream at me ever again. What is unfortunate is that besides the "report" meetings, our work relationship was a positive one. After I reached my breaking point, her yelling stopped. but she was more withdrawn in her interactions with me. I never figured out why it was O.K. for her to treat me poorly, but when I finally found my voice it bruised her so badly that she couldn't recover from it.

I left the organization within six months after that meeting.

A.R.T.less leaders can cause all kinds of problems for themselves, their teams, and for the organizations they work for. The 10 Flaws in this chapter are just some of the flaws that diminish the opportunity for leaders to lead A.R.T.fully. Do you recognize any of these flaws in your own leadership style? Do you see yourself in any of the stories? If so, don't beat yourself up. I invite you to start taking steps toward being an A.R.T.ful Leader. It's a process that begins with recognizing the need to make a change.

Remember my story? The relationship with my son began to change when I recognized my own Flaw. We all want to be more effective leaders in our work and in all the other leadership roles we play. Trust me on this, and read on where you will learn specific ways to begin to be perceived as a leader who is not flawed, but as a leader who leads with A.R.T.ful intention.

A.R.T.ful Leadership Reflection Journal

1. Have you ever had a leader who exhibited any of these A.R.T.less leadership flaws? If so, which ones? List them and describe the impact they had on you and on your team's effectiveness. What have you learned from this experience that you are committed to avoid in your own leadership journey?

2. Have you ever or are you currently demonstrating any of the A.R.T.less leadership Flaws? If so which ones? (Try to answer this as honestly as possible. Be daring and ask someone you A.R.T. for feedback.) What actions can you take to reverse this trend in order to get on the track to A.R.T.ful Leadership?

Admiration, Respect, and Trust

The remainder of *A.R.T.Ful Leadership: The Path to be Admired, Respected, and Trusted as a Leader* is dedicated to providing a practical approach to what it takes for a leader to be perceived as an A.R.T.ful Leader. A chapter is dedicated to each of the three A.R.T.ful Leadership elements. The key Drivers for A.R.T.ful Leadership will be revisited and expanded to include the critical Attributes (behaviors) linked to each of the Drivers. These Attributes are concrete actions (some may call these skills or competencies) that when mastered, will begin to increase you're A.R.T.ful Leadership capability.

As you review each Driver it is recommended that you evaluate your own capabilities in each of the Drivers and associated Attributes. You may have already have mastered some, while in others you have work left to do. Where you have mastered certain Attributes, this should validate your leadership capability. Review the suggestions for potential new ideas to "polish the brass," so to speak. In the areas that you have not mastered, take time to consider how to focus on those Attributes and begin to improve in those areas. I urge you not to ignore or mentally argue that any of the Drivers or Attributes are not necessary or needed in your particular case. Certain Drivers and associated Attributes may seem very foreign to you, maybe very uncomfortable for you to explore and begin to master. That is a natural response to growth. The key is to not ignore any of the Drivers or any of the Attributes. Collectively, they lead to A.R.T.ful Leadership.

Finally, there will be considerable times throughout that you will be challenged by *Reflection Journal Activities*. These include a series of questions that will ask you to reflect on your past leadership experiences, both being led and leading. Take the time to complete each of these reflections. It is critical to your A.R.T.ful Leadership Journey. Keep a notebook close at hand to record all the "reflections" in one place. A.R.T.ful Leadership is an intentional act. Your *Reflection Journal Activities* will be incredibly helpful to you.

Note: A compendium workbook is available that provides resources, worksheets, and tools to assist you in completing the A.R.T.ful Leadership Journal Activities. Visit www.art-fulleadership.com for details.

Admiration

I have always been an admirer. I regard the gift
of admiration as indispensable if one is to amount to something;
I don't know where I would be without it.

Francois de La Rochefoucauld

Know yourself. Don't accept your dog's admiration as
conclusive evidence that you are wonderful.

Ann Landers

Admiration: To have a high opinion of a leader by virtue of what a leader
is able to deliver to the organization, function, and team. Leaders who
are admired are looked up to by those they lead due to the ability of the
leader to act with integrity and connect to individuals.

I want to describe Admiration in A.R.T.ful Leadership in the context of *Intimate Admiration*. This means that individuals have a direct relationship with the leader. *Intimate Admiration* results in individuals reaching their own conclusions (or their own perceptions) of a leader through direct contact. Perception is not built solely from what others say about the leader, what the leader says about themselves (in a public forum), what they read about the leader in an organization medium, or read in some other electronic medium. None of those are "intimate." Personal contact is needed for someone to make his or her own evaluation of the leader. Simply put, *Intimate Admiration* is *knowing* the leader.

Why is Intimate Admiration important? Over the years I have admired several leaders from afar. I remember being nervous when I would get the opportunity to meet some of them. After all, I thought highly of them; many were high-powered extremely powerful (in the business sense) individuals. There were times (thankfully, years ago) when I would work myself into such a complete frenzy that I would not make a good impression. Sometimes after I met a particular leader or worked with his or her leadership team and intimately had an opportunity to get to *know* the leader, admiration flew out the window.

At the same time I have also been joyously pleased at meeting other leaders (Ken Blanchard being one) who could not have met and exceeded my expectations more. Other encounters actually started off poorly but then leaders intentionally worked to change how they were perceived at first (some with my influence). Those are the leaders whom I applaud the most—for recognizing that an opportunity existed to improve A.R.T.ful Leadership and took responsibility to intentionally change and improve how they were being perceived.

Through many such contacts, observations, and experiences, I have learned that Intimate Admiration is critical in formulating the perception of A.R.T.ful Leadership. You can't rely on nor should you *believe everything that you hear,* either positive or negative. Make the determination yourself. And as leaders, ensure that those whom you lead and influence have the ability to have access—Intimate Access—to you as a leader. And when they do, seize those opportunities.

ADMIRE DRIVERS

Note: *Skilled Communicator* impacts the ability to be perceived as A.R.T.ful in each of the three elements of the A.R.T.ful Leadership Model. Therefore, Skilled Communicator will be infused in the discussion of each of the Drivers and associated Attributes as applicable.

Admire Drivers: Definitions

The key drivers that define a leader as Admired are defined in the following way:

Deliver Consistent Results: An admired leader delivers consistent results to the organization. This requires *devising* a *sound strategy* and *executing* on that strategy with and through others *flawlessly*.

Competent: An admired leader is well-versed in the industry and possesses a deep business knowledge. Has the ability to demonstrate leadership capability (in leading people). Demonstrates a tenacious drive to succeed and motivate others.

Social Dexterity: An admired leader is adept at connecting with people and building a wide network both at an organizational level and at a social level. At ease in a variety of situations and contexts. Perceived as someone who can freely engage others in conversation.

Authentic: An admired leader demonstrates empathy and has a clear moral compass. Is self-assured and able to show vulnerability. Makes an effort to connect with individuals on an interpersonal level and cultivate interpersonal relationships.

Represents with Credibility: An admired leader is able to represent the organization, function, and team with the utmost credibility. Builds this impression with constituents both inside and outside the organization.

Skilled Communicator: An admired leader communicates openly and honestly. Delivers information with ease and confidence. Answers the "why" for individuals in order for people to understand the rationale for decisions that have been made by the leader and/or organization. Allows and encourages open dialogue and exchanges to drive ideas forward.

Admire Drivers: Key Attributes

Each of the Admire Drivers have related Attributes that contribute to a leader being perceived as Admired by those they lead and influence. Each Attribute is described to provide an understanding of the behaviors that lead to Admiration.

Driver: Delivering Consistent Results

ELEMENT	DRIVER	ATTRIBUTES
Admiration	Deliver Consistent Results	1 > Strategy 2 > Operational Plan 3 > Execute Flawlessly

Delivering Consistent Results is consistently mentioned by participants in our studies as one of the key drivers that contributes to a leader being perceived as Admired. This should come as no surprise. If you aren't delivering results, you are unlikely to be perceived or received very well by your team or anyone else of importance in the organization for long. Organizations have placed greater and greater importance on this driver over the years as the focus on profits and bottom-line results has increased tremendously. In fact, to the detriment of A.R.T.ful Leadership, this is the only driver that matters in some organizations. When this is the case, it is no wonder that A.R.T.less leadership starts and stops with this driver.

When an organization is focused exclusively on delivering consistent results and disregards other key leadership drivers A.R.T.ful Leadership will not be achieved. When an organization is entirely focused on this single driver it is not balanced and is not focused on creating true synergy (as you will see in an upcoming chapter).

In the pursuit of bottom-line results the tone of the organization and the culture of the organization become overly competitive. Don't get me wrong; competition is terrific. But when competition breeds bad behavior, it is counterproductive to collaboration, saps energy, lowers productivity, and pits organizational members against one another. It does not serve the organization well. Time and time again I have seen that focusing on this driver alone (including organizational policies and practices that only reward this driver) will deprive an organization from having a culture that is vibrant; it just simply doesn't happen. (If you think you have an example of a vibrant company that has delivering results as its sole driver, please contact me and prove me wrong. I trust my phone will not ring).

A.R.T.ful Leaders understand that it is only by working *with and through people that results can be consistently delivered.* Consistent results are not achieved or sustained by working against individuals, going behind their backs, or pitting organizational members against one another to get ahead. A.R.T.less leaders use such behaviors to deliver results. Bottom-line results may be positively impacted for a time, but the negative impact these competitive tactics have when used to achieve results are sometimes horrific.

A.R.T.ful Leaders who were perceived to deliver consistent results demonstrated the following Attributes:

Conceive sound **strategy**
Convert that strategy into sound **operational plans**
Execute flawlessly

Attribute 1 > Strategy
Creating a sound strategy requires the following elements:

Mission: Having a clear understanding and commitment to the mission of the organization. Understanding the core business of the organization provides focus and direction for individuals inside and outside the organization. This requires a leader to know the organization's purpose for being—its fundamental mission.

Vision: The vision of the organization that is aligned with its mission sets the bar for where the organization will be in the future. A vision provides a future focus that the organization is driving to achieve through the strategy.

Understanding customers: The organization must know and serve its current customers in order to keep them, and discover how to capture future customers.

Market forces: Scanning the external environment and analyzing all market forces that influence the organization play a significant role in strategy formulation—including what goals are set, what markets to enter, and how to utilize resources.

Organizational capability: Analyzing and determining the capabilities of the organization enable the organization to be successful and avoid the barriers that may impede future success.

Critical questions to answer during strategy formulation include the following:
- What is the mission and vision of the organization?
- What are your core products and services? What are the market dynamics of each? Which products and services do we want to explore?

- Who are our customers? What do they want? How will their needs change over the next __ years? Who don't we have as customers that we want as customers, and why don't they do business with us currently?
- Who are our competitors? What do we do better than our competitors? What do our competitors do better than us?
- What are our organizational capabilities? What are our resource strengths and barriers? Where do performance issues exist?

If you were asked to answer the above questions regarding your current strategy, could you answer them? If so, congratulations. This is often not the case, except for a few within an organization. Many leaders, it seems, rely on a tactical rather than a strategic approach to leadership. However, tactics done without a strategy will only prove that you are doing a lot, but whether or not you are truly making strategic progress may be unclear. Without a blueprint that a strategy provides, actions may fall short or drain organizational resources.

A Personal Look at a Lack of Strategy

My wife often asks me if I know where we are going when we get in the car to head for an event. I often say "yes" when I actually don't have a clue exactly where I am going. I know the general vicinity, so off I go anyway. As I arrive in the general area (or sometimes not), and realize that I am hopelessly lost, I remain silent. When I realize that I have gone too far and need to backtrack, I sneakily attempt to turn around without my wife noticing. This is when my wife will say, "Oh look, surprise, surprise, we are in a parking lot." This is the standard phrase for "we are lost." Thank goodness for GPS. I never leave home without mine, and this has reduced my time in strange parking lots.

This is an example of taking action without a strategy. A lack of strategy may take you in the general right direction, but without clearly knowing where you are going you will likely have to take corrective action that will be a drain on time and resources.

When devising a strategy, our studies are clear that leaders who are inclusive in their approach to strategy formulation are Admired. Leaders must tap into the intellectual property readily available to them both inside and outside the organization. Leaders who do not take advantage of the opportunity to engage others in formulating a strategy, particularly those who are challenging the status quo, driving organizational change, and inventing and reinventing will miss the best ideas that a strategy should contain. The biggest mistake leadership makes is devising strategy in a vacuum by closing themselves in the boardroom. Without a feedback loop at some level and without engaging the organization, organizational strategy will not resonate with the individuals who are tasked with executing the strategy.

Attribute 2 > Operational Plan

Operational plans are short-term in nature with the intent to achieve specific goals that satisfy certain components of the overall strategy. Operational plans must be *effective* ("doing the right things") to succeed in achieving goals. The right tactics (actions) must be identified that will achieve organizational goals. Each tactic must carefully be aligned with the proper resources (people, technologies), located in the right location.

Attribute 3 > Execute Flawlessly

Once the plan is in place, it must be executed flawlessly to be *efficient* ("doing things right"). This requires a leader having the proper level of checks and balances to monitor execution. This also requires a leader to have the agility to adapt to changes in the environment and to adapt the plan without being completely knocked off course.

Communication

The final component of strategy that is fundamental is *communication.* Is the strategy of the company communicated to the organization? Is the strategy understood? Do the organization members understand their individual roles and responsibilities in contributing to the strategy? Answering these questions is the direct responsibility of leaders.

Our studies have found that many organizational members unfortunately are not aware of the strategy of their organizations (at any level—neither the organization's strategy nor the function's strategy). Some organizational members conclude that the organization doesn't have a strategy or assume that the strategy must be flawed since it hasn't been shared. Communicating strategy is key to ensuring that organizational members understand their role in the big picture of organizational success. Too often strategy stops at the senior level, and marching orders are simply delivered to the front-line. That is not the best means to create and sustain an energized workforce that is working together toward a common goal.

"You Have Got to Be Kidding Me"
A Story of Lack of Strategy and Admiration

Recently my division has gone through some major changes. New executive leadership, changing roles, and organizational structure: you name it, it has happened. As a leader in the organization I have been trying to figure out what all the changes mean to my role in the organization going forward and what it means to my team. However, it would seem that no one is adding clarity to the situation. This isn't helping my ability to lead. My team is continuously asking me to clarify where we are going and clarify the new structure. I keep telling them to be patient and that I will let them know as soon as I hear anything, but their patience is growing thin.

Operational planning and the budget planning cycle are right around the corner. This is the time I have to plan the coming year's actions and to determine the financial support needed to achieve the department goals. But without an understanding of the wider strategy of the division I am at a loss, particularly in light of all the changes in the organization. The clock has been ticking now for four months since the changes, and the new executive leader has remained elusive except for calling me into the office from time to time to tell me to do specific tasks.

Last week I scheduled a meeting with the leader to get clarity on where we were heading. The leader doesn't like meetings and avoids them. In fact the leadership team only meets once a month, which hardly seems to be enough in this time of change. And during those meetings it is clear the leadership team is not to ask questions—it is not appropriate. But, I couldn't stand it anymore.

So I sat down with the leader and expressed in very general terms my concerns. Trust me; I was extremely careful in the choice of words I used. I then said that I was preparing to create the operational plan for the coming year. I explained that I was anxious to get started and needed guidance to help me get started. Then I asked this question, "What is your overall strategy for the division?" And I waited . . . and waited . . . and waited. The leader stared at me without saying a word for what seemed like an eternity. I held my tongue, although I felt like talking to stop the silence. I just sat there and stared back.

My leader finally replied, "The strategy will play itself out over time."

I thought to myself, "You have got to be kidding me! No strategy? So what is the basis of my operational plan? My operational plan should be based on what exactly?"

I had all these questions but didn't dare ask any of them. I continued, pushing a bit to gain clarity, "Well, what are your thoughts concerning the direction of the function? In light of the realignment it would appear that there may be a different direction that you intend to take and responsibilities may shift. If that is the case, it would potentially have a significant impact on my operational plan. So if you could speak to that it would be incredibly helpful." The leader again just looked at me.

What followed was a bunch of talk with no substance. What I got out of it was that the leader would tell me what to do and when to do it. I left the office knowing less then when I entered, except that the function was now at a place where we had absolutely no strategy whatsoever. I also decided that I would not turn in an operational plan until I was asked to do one. And when and if I was asked for one, I would have to ask what it should include, since I had no idea what my department actually was responsible for any longer.

During the conversation I did ask if the leader would be planning a strategy session with the leadership team in the future. The response was that none was planned.

Time to dust off my resume, I do believe.

Driver: Competent

ELEMENT	DRIVER	ATTRIBUTES
Admiration	Competent	4 > Knowledgeable 5 > Leadership Aptitude 6 > Tenacious Drive to Succeed

Leaders who are perceived as Competent are leaders who possess deep knowledge of the industry and business. Competent leaders have an aptitude to lead. They not only hold a leadership position; they are actually perceived as a leader. Competent leaders also have a tenacious drive to succeed and facilitate others to succeed by setting an example and motivating others.

Attribute 4 > Knowledgeable

Demonstrating industry knowledge is highly admired by organizational members. Organizational members seem to continuously assess whether or not their leader actually knows what is going on (in the industry, organization, and function). If they conclude that the leader isn't knowledgeable, admiration wanes.

A leader must be intentional in keeping their team informed regarding the industry. Keeping team members informed about things of interest in the industry and about items that may impact the business is an essential component for a leader to be perceived as knowledgeable. A leader's team is always looking for a leader to provide that lens.

Leaders must be knowledgeable of the division or function they lead. This means knowing how the function works, as well as the roles and responsibilities that comprise the function. Leaders must know what is "top of mind" for the team members within their organization, including what is working and what challenges team members face. When a leader lacks this knowledge—doesn't know how the work is accomplished nor the challenges the team faces—then the leader is merely relegated to figurehead by team members. A figurehead leader lacks the ability to contribute in a meaningful way and is perceived as not adding value as the leader of the function.

There have been countless times in working with teams when I have heard statements such as, "My leader is out of touch." "My leader doesn't have a clue what really is going on with our customers." "My leader doesn't care about us." "Our leader doesn't know what we do." These comments are indicators that the leader lacks knowledge of the function they lead and therefore is not able to influence and create true and sustained followership.

Attribute 5 > Leadership Aptitude

It is interesting indeed that Leadership Aptitude is consistently mentioned as an attribute of an Admired leader. Leadership, in the broadest terms is reflected throughout the A.R.T.ful Leadership Model. So, it was imperative to distinguish Leadership Aptitude in the context of Delivering Consistent Results.

Leadership Aptitude in relation to Delivering Consistent Results consists of the following behaviors:

Leadership Agility and Adaptability: Leaders must first demonstrate leadership agility and adaptability. Leaders do this by continuously analyzing progress against plans and adjusting as necessary in order to keep the organization moving forward with as little disruption as possible. This also takes the form of a leader being able to be adaptive to new ideas and incorporate those ideas to optimize organizational productivity. And throughout all of this, a leader must possess a temperament that is A.R.T.ful. This means that the leader is able to lead change and motivate others to adapt without creating organizational strain and chaos. I have witnessed and have heard many leaders who lack this critical attribute. Yelling from the corner office or acting like Chicken Little (falsely predicting doom and gloom) does not demonstrate true *agility* or *adaptability*.

Leading Teams and Individuals: Leaders must be adept at leading teams and individuals. One of the ways this translates is through the ability to provide clear direction and instruction to the entire team and to individuals alike. Without clarity, execution will fall short. Often when directions and instructions are not clear team members will not question or challenge. Instead, they will just walk away confused and try to gain clarification amongst themselves. They will then *hope* that what they do meets expectations–not an ideal situation. A colleague of mine calls it "The impossible game." Leaders need to take ownership for how they communicate and follow through on this responsibility. Communication needs to be deliberate, clear, and succinct if you hope to have everyone on the same page, desire to create buy-in, and achieve organizational alignment. Consider this: when we ask leaders if they communicate to their teams enough, the majority say "yes." When we ask team members the same question, a resounding majority (above 80%), indicate communication is lacking or poor from their leaders. Someone doesn't have an accurate picture of what is actually going on.

Without communication, leaders will not be perceived as possessing *leadership aptitude*. This is another reason why the Communication Driver influences each element within the A.R.T.ful Leadership Model.

"Crazy Town"
Story of a Lack of Knowledge or Leadership Competency

My peers are high-level professionals with a great deal of responsibility. We each have very specific clients and are responsible for ensuring those clients' needs are met. Unfortunately, our leader, and I use the term very loosely, does not know anything about our role and what we do (what competencies are required to be successful).

It would seem that the leader was placed in the position due to her ability to manage up. It seems to me and my peers that is the only way our leader could have possibly gotten the job. It certainly wasn't based on competency. So, she doesn't know our role, but is she a good leader? To that I must answer, No, no, no, no, no.

During team meetings my peers and I suffer through agendas that are not relevant to what we do and are forced to try and engage in discussions that are a huge waste of time. We speak of this often and grumble about having to go to meetings. After the meetings we gather around the water cooler and talk about how crazy the meetings are.

Then there are the dreaded one-on-ones. Wow, those are painful. Our leader, the poor thing, tries to validate her position by having us talk about the various projects we are executing. Then she tries to provide suggestions for us to incorporate. Mind you, her suggestions lack any sense of reality or lack any smidgen of value. I hate to be mean, but it is just the fact. If on occasion (once every fourth month) she does have a suggestion that might be relevant, she is so out of touch with what we do, she doesn't realize that the suggestion is far too little far too late to be considered.

When I or my peers attempt to explain why her suggestions are not particularly helpful (in as nicest terms as possible), it just serves to prolong the discussion. At the end of each of our one-on-ones we gather around the water cooler once again to lament about how painful each of our experiences has been and how crazy it is. And that brings me to my point.

Over time she became known as "Crazy Town" in my group. Now, that is not a very nice nickname, I know. After all, who would like to be known as Crazy Town (except perhaps unless you were living in a frat house). We try and avoid her at all costs. We plan project meetings to avoid coming to team meetings and we schedule client meetings back-to-back in order to skip some of our one-on-ones. Crazy Town may not be a very nice nickname, but it fits her to a tee. She lacks knowledge and leadership skills. She doesn't add value, and when she opens her mouth crazy stuff comes out. Poor Crazy Town and more importantly, poor us.

Attribute 6 > Tenacious Drive to Succeed

Leaders who demonstrate a tenacious drive to succeed do so by demonstrating positivity, a strong work ethic, and making tough decisions when needed.

Positivity: Positivity is demonstrated by remaining upbeat and positive when interacting with the team. This includes remaining positive even in the times of organizational uncertainty. During these times a leader will set the tone that will carry through the rest of the organization. A positive approach that communicates encouragement and a sense of determined purpose during challenging times will provide team members with a renewed determination. Leaders who are unable to remain visible during difficult times or who don't energize the organization will be perceived with little admiration. A leader who is not excited about what is happening in the organization should not be surprised that the organization is not excited either. As John C. Maxwell states, "When a leader reaches out in passion, he is usually met with an answering passion."[1] Positivity and passion are accomplished through a leader's ability to *communicate* effectively both verbally and nonverbally. Positivity and passion communicated effectively is infectious.

Work Ethic: Leaders should be perceived as having the strongest work ethic within their team. This doesn't mean that the leader can't have a balanced life (quite the contrary). This means the leader demonstrates a commitment to the organization and a commitment to the success of the team as well. A leader sets the tone for the work ethic of the individuals they lead. A.R.T.ful Leadership is about demonstrating to the organization how to work smarter and faster. A leader that is perceived as someone who is able to manage the various demands of the organization and also can maintain a balance within their lives is perceived much more favorably then a leader who is only driven by leading the organization. This trait is more important than ever before, especially with the younger age groups in the workforce who are the leaders of tomorrow and are no longer interested in sacrificing their entire life to an organization. It isn't just about working hard; it is about working hard and smart.

Making Tough Decisions: Leaders who are perceived as having a tenacious drive for success also display the resolve to make tough decisions and to stick by the decisions once made. Leaders must demonstrate the courage to step forward without hesitation and make decisions in times when decisions need to be made to move the organization forward. Just as important is a leader's ability to clearly communicate the decision along with the rationale for the decision and how the decision will be executed. Answering the "why" behind the decision is key to organizational understanding and gaining buy-in. The leader who has strong decision-making ability is an Admired leader.

Driver: Social Dexterity

ELEMENT	DRIVER	ATTRIBUTES
Admiration	Social Dexterity	7 > Networking

Leaders who possess Social Dexterity have the ability to network with a wide range of individuals inside and outside the organization. Through interpersonal communication, leaders with social dexterity are at ease in a variety of social and business situations. The ability to converse and find interest in others conveys a sense that they are genuinely interested in others. Leaders with Social Dexterity freely engage others in conversations and demonstrate genuine interest in what others have to say. Individuals with Social Dexterity will engage in transactional conversations rather than controlling conversations.

Attribute 7 > Networking

Building relationships is the result of a leader having the ability to connect with people and create both business and social networks. Relationship building is done by living with a sense of curiosity, having interest in others, and engaging people in conversation. If this doesn't come naturally, and to some it doesn't, a leader needs to be intentional in developing this skill. The ability to be comfortable in a variety of situations and contexts and comfortably engage others in conversation is critical in building relationships.

- If you are not comfortable in engaging in small talk, get comfortable. Practice. If you are an introvert (trust me, I know), push yourself. Develop five to ten questions that you can use as conversation starters. This will help to engage others in conversation. Questions should include both business and professional questions and those that are interpersonal in nature.
- Focus on others, not yourself. Relationship building is about being interested in what someone else has to say. If you are self-absorbed it is a relationship destroyer. Learn to extend yourself beyond—you. Learn to listen and live curious. This may be counter to a leader's well-developed ego.
- Once you have established a connection, keep the connection active. Relationships take work in our personal lives, and this is no different in our professional lives.

Driver: Authentic

ELEMENT	DRIVER	ATTRIBUTES
Admiration	Authentic	8 > Confidence 9 > Connecting 10 > Compatibility

Much research has been conducted regarding Authentic Leadership—what it is, what it takes, the skills required, and much more. When exploring the drivers and attributes of an A.R.T.ful Leader it was not surprising that being authentic was linked to Admiration. The approach here is not to create a new definition of authentic leadership nor to borrow a definition from the myriad of leadership content that is available. The key for the A.R.T.ful Leadership Model was to identify the authentic attributes that contribute to a leader being Admired. In our studies, there are three characteristics that set authentic leaders apart from inauthentic leaders. In A.R.T.ful Leadership terms Authentic Leaders possess the 3C's: Confidence, the ability to Connect, and the ability to be Compatible with others.

Attribute 8 > Confidence

Leaders who project confidence and self-assurance are perceived as authentic. People can *see* and *feel* a leader who is comfortable in his or her own skin. A leader who isn't confident and self-assured will tend to be viewed less favorably, and team members pick up on this awkwardness.

Leaders who are lacking in confidence and self-assurance tend to lead from afar. They prefer to lead via email rather than in person. They do not engage with their team, because it is just too painful to do so. Additionally, leaders who lack confidence tend to put on a "leader" persona (I know a leader who always introduces himself by his title, no matter how many times you meet him). A confident and self-assured leader is one who's very presence demands attention through natural charisma.

Attribute 9 > Connections

Admired Leaders are those who can connect with people at an individual and personal level. When leaders possess Social Dexterity, it is likely that Connections will be quite easy to achieve. Recall the story in Chapter 1 of the CEO Michael Howe who was upset about realizing he did not now everyone's name because the organization had grown so large. This is a tremendous example of a leader who has the ability to *connect*.

Leaders who establish connections make those around them feel as though they are important and valued. In turn, leaders will be rewarded by increased commitment and increased motivation by those they lead, and increased devotion by those they influence. The ability to Connect is core to A.R.T.ful Leadership.

Attribute 10 > Compatibility

Someone once articulated compatibility this way: "It is a leader knowing who he is and others knowing what to expect from him." That is it, pure and simple. As a leader, do your people know who you are as a leader and what they can expect from you? Or, are your people on edge when they are in your presence? How accurately you are able to answer these questions will determine how compatible you are with those you lead and influence.

When you are able to connect authentically with people, everything becomes more fluid. On the other hand, if your compatibility is low, everything is more difficult; communication is arduous, buy-in is difficult to achieve, and collaboration is nonexistent.

How open the communication climate is between the leader and organizational members will be the key indicator on the compatibility quotient that exists within an organization. An open communication climate allows freedom to share information without filtering. It doesn't matter who you are or what you say; the key is that you communicate because what you say has value and is important to the organization.

If you don't let people in, people will not let you in; it is that simple. To personalize this, I think that if you were to ask those who I have worked closely with over the years, many would say that I am authentic, and they would also say that I am a little crazy (which I also admit proudly). If you asked them why they think I am authentic they would immediately begin to tell you detailed information about me—my likes and dislikes, what I am passionate about. They would be able to name my family and tell you specifics about them (sometimes too many specifics if you asked my children), and they would share stories that I have shared with them. That ability to build compatibility leads to being perceived as authentic.

Admiration Driver: Credibility

ELEMENT	DRIVER	ATTRIBUTES
Admiration	Credibility	11 > High Moral Compass 12 > Values 13 > Integrity 14 > Reputation

The last driver that contributes to a leader being viewed as Admired is Credibility. Credibility is a result of a leader being a credible representative of the organization, division, and function. As a leader, you are the "face" of those you lead and are an extension of your team. How you represent your constituents directly impacts the reputation of those you lead. One result of the alleged sex abuse scandal that made headlines in 2011 at Penn State was a 40 percent drop in sales of products with the Penn State logo.[2] This is an example of how credibility, or lack thereof, can hurt the organization's reputation.

Organization members watch leaders constantly. This means leadership comes with a tremendous obligation to act with credibility. Not only do organizational members watch leaders, they watch leaders with a very critical eye. Leaders who pass the test will be viewed with a high-degree of credibility; those who fall short will be viewed with little credibility and lack Admiration.

Attribute 11 > High Moral Compass

Acting with credibility requires a leader to possess a high moral compass. Leaders must demonstrate sound judgment and be steadfast in doing what is right for the organization and for individuals they serve. Without a strong moral compass a leader will lack credibility.

Attribute 12 > Values

Leaders must be clear about what is important to them. What a leader values is important for organizational members to understand, and a leader needs to communicate their values to the organization. When a leader's values are clear, team members understand who the leader is and how the leader will lead. Leading by values is a mark of a principled leader. In addition, communicating values sets expectations regarding acceptable behavior within the organization.

Leaders also need to be cognizant of whether or not their personal values are in alignment with the values of the organization. If a leader is not aligned with organizational values, that leader will have a difficult time being perceived as credible, and a strain will be placed on working relationships. Leaders must take the time to assess whether their individual values are in concert with organizational values, and if not, they may be personally conflicted in leading A.R.T.fully.

Values are a clear attribute of a leader being perceived as authentic. Value clarity, value alignment, and conviction to lead by values will increase your credibility and contribute to being perceived as an Admired leader.

Attribute 13 > Integrity

Leaders need to be sure their actions are consistent with their words. When they are not, then integrity does not exist. Say what you are going to do, and do what you say. That is the true test of a leader who acts with integrity. Without integrity, your team and organization will not trust you. They will decide they cannot depend on you or rely on you, and they will begin to ignore you as a leader. When a leader lacks integrity, they lack any hope of influencing. Integrity is paramount to being viewed as credible.

Attribute 14 > Reputation

When you are not around, what do people say about you? Do people speak highly of you? How do they describe you? What do they say about your ability to represent them? How do they describe your ability to lead? In their eyes, do you act with integrity? What do people say about your credibility? What is the reputation that you have been able to create as the face of the organization? Do leaders and customers look forward to working with you? Does your team look forward to working with you, or do they cringe at the thought of meeting with you? The answers to all these questions will determine the reputation YOU have created.

Your reputation precedes you. Your reputation impacts your effectiveness. Can you lead without a good reputation? Yes, but not A.R.T.fully. The reputation that you have created allows you access to information (or blocks you from information). A good reputation attracts people to you; a poor reputation repels people away. The goal of A.R.T.ful Leadership is to create and sustain true followership by those you lead and influence. This requires a superior reputation and credibility to achieve this goal.

The Merger
A Story of Admiration

There were rumors that our beloved CEO was leaving the company. The rumors had been heating up for the past month. I simply couldn't believe it, although the past couple of weeks the CEO had become less and less visible. I attributed it to being really busy, while others attributed his absence to setting the stage to pass the reigns to new leadership. Then last week, without any notice, we all received an email. Management was being required to gather all their staff within an hour for an announcement. I feared the time was here.

We had been acquired by a much larger company about six months prior. It appeared they wanted our company to expand their visibility in the market. At first it sounded like a great opportunity. Our parent company had many resources, and were committed to support our growth and allow us to remain autonomous since they did not operate in our space prior to purchasing the company. In all meetings with executives from the new parent company and with our own executive leadership the message was that it would be "business as usual" for the next five years. But this meeting seemed to signal that maybe something had changed.

People entered the room without saying a word. You could feel the tension in the air. I immediately noticed that our CEO was seated at the front of the room along with three others, the COO from the parent company, the head of our board of directors, and one other person I had never seen before.

I can't explain how our CEO looked. He was not himself. Our CEO was always extremely positive and exuded high energy. If you were around him and were not in a particularly good mood, that wouldn't last long. He would pick up on it and immediately start working on you to turn things around—always in a positive way. He always had a smile on his face. Today was a different. I realized the rumors were true. When you looked around the room you could see that everyone else realized what was going on before the meeting started.

The meeting began by the COO of the parent company giving a brief statement that said that he appreciated us taking time out of our day . . . yadda, yadda, yadda. Finally, he said that our CEO had decided to leave the company and seek other opportunities. He thanked our CEO for all his contributions (though it sounded as if he didn't believe a word of it) and sat down.

If you knew all the rumors (which I have found are often more accurate than what you hear officially), they included that our CEO was being forced out, that he was under a great deal of pressure to change operations dramatically—including how our company did business—and that our CEO was resisting because these changes did not make sense. According to the rumors, it came down to a power struggle that resulted in our CEO being forced out and replaced with a new CEO from the parent company.

Our CEO stood up and tried to break the tension with a flippant comment (as usual) but it really didn't work. I noticed that several people in the room were crying. He talked about what a privilege it was to lead all of us, what a tremendous opportunity it was to work with each of us to grow the company the past several years, and that an opportunity still exists to continue the vision that had been established at the company. He talked about what a tremendous partnership there was with the parent company (and it really sounded genuine) and that we had to move forward and learn how to partner effectively with the parent company. He thanked us many, many times for our hard work. He then introduced the new CEO (the person I didn't know). He talked about the new CEO's experience and how lucky we were to have him as the new CEO. He also said he was going to stick around for as long as needed to ensure a smooth transition.

I admired him greatly for his ability to have the courage to do what he did, namely to stick with the vision of what we had built to date and to commend us for all we had accomplished. As usual, his message was about us, not him; about the company and not about his loss; about keeping us connected and committed to the vision even as he departed. It was just like him. It was deeply personal and was inspiring.

What surprised me is that when the meeting was over everyone started to file out of the room, and no one was going to the front of the room to talk to our CEO. I did. I walked up, I gave the CEO a hand shake and then a hug and I said, "I am so sorry." He whispered, "Let's get the hell out of here." I realized then that the rumors had been true. That he was putting a good face on a bad situation as he needed to do for the organization and the employees. I also realized how very difficult it was for him to do what he had just done and how painful the last few weeks must have been for him. I also realized that this meeting was his idea, because if it was up to the parent company (as I learned very soon), there would have been a short announcement or perhaps no announcement at all—which is common when leaders are replaced or leave the company.

Me? I did get the hell out of there shortly thereafter.

A.R.T.ful Leadership Reflection Journal

1. What leader have you Admired and why? What can you learn from their leadership that you can incorporate in your own leadership journey?

2. Which of the Admiration Drivers and Attributes do you need to strengthen?

3. Who Admires you as a leader?

4. Who is critical for your success as a leader but may not Admire you? Why? What steps can you take to begin to change that perception?

Respect

I don't think I have been loved by my troops,
but I think I have been respected.
William Westmoreland

Respect: To feel genuine appreciation and gratitude towards a leader. Individuals appreciate the leader for the mutual respect the leader shows to others and the energy the leader provides to ensure individuals and the team are successful.

The second element of A.R.T.ful Leadership is *Respect*. Respect is earned. It does not come from a person's title or position. Think about it from your own point of view. Who have you respected as a leader, or who do you respect as a leader? What have the leaders that come to mind done to earn the respect you have for them? Is it because they held a leadership position, or did they earn your respect through their actions and intentions? I am certain your respect has to do with how they acted as a leader and not simply from the role or title that they had in an organization.

Leaders earn the respect of those they lead by benefiting the people they lead, through offering guidance and wisdom, and through the example they set. Individuals can respect a position (Presidency or CEO of a corporation), but they may not respect the individual who holds the position because of their actions. Therefore, Respect is earned through what you do as a leader, not by who you are or what your position says you are.

Research indicates that individuals respect leaders when they view the leader as committed to their success by how the leader interacts and leads the team. The "R" in A.R.T.ful Leadership can be summed up by a quote from H. Gordon Selfridge who was a pioneer in the retail industry (Marshall Field and Company). "The boss drives people; the leader coaches them. The boss depends on authority; the leader on good will. The boss inspires fear; the leader inspires enthusiasm. The boss says "I"; The leader says "WE." The boss fixes the blame for the breakdown; the leader fixes the breakdown. The boss says, "GO"; the leader says "LET'S GO!"

RESPECT DRIVERS

RESPECT

Supportive
Demonstrate Mutual Respect
Responsible and Accountable
Provides Feedback and Counsel
Fair and Balanced

SKILLED COMMUNICATOR

Note: *Skilled Communicator* impacts the ability to be perceived as A.R.T.ful in each of the three elements of the A.R.T.ful Leadership Model. Therefore, Skilled Communicator will be infused in the discussion of each of the Drivers and associated Attributes as applicable.

Respect Drivers: Definitions

The key drivers that define a leader as Respected focus on a leader's ability to interact positively with those they lead and influence and impart leadership wisdom. The five Respect Drivers and the Skilled Communicator Driver that influences each element of A.R.T.ful Leadership are defined as follows:

Supportive: A respected leader consistently demonstrates loyalty to team members and stakeholders. Provides assistance, information, and encouragement as needed for the function to be successful.

Demonstrate Mutual Respect: A respected leader demonstrates mutual respect by being approachable by all levels within an organization. Shows genuine interest in what everyone, regardless of level in the organization, has to offer and contribute to the organization.

Responsible and Accountable: A respected leader sets clear performance expectations and holds themselves and others accountable.

Provide Feedback and Counsel: A respected leader is adept at providing feedback on a continuous basis and views feedback as a necessary component for success. Seeks feedback and provides needed feedback.

Fair and Balanced: A respected leader provides opportunities, rewards, and recognition to all members of the organization and team. Diligently treats individuals fairly and consistently (avoiding being perceived as having organizational favorites when rewarding, recognizing, and promoting individuals).

Skilled Communicator: Being a skilled communicator is core to demonstrating the Respect Driver. The respected leader communicates *support* and delivers *feedback*. Establishes clear *expectations*, demonstrates *mutual respect* through interactions and demonstrates fairness through open and honest communications.

Respect Drivers: Key Attributes

The Respect Drivers each have attributes (behaviors) that have been identified to impact how a leader is perceived. Leaders who master these attributes and incorporate them into their daily interactions with those they lead and influence will be perceived with Respect. Consistently demonstrating these attributes into your leadership increases your Respect quotient (the degree to which you are perceived as a respected leader). Each of these attributes is described below to help you assess your own respect quotient. As you review the respect drivers and attributes continuously ask the questions: Who respects me as a leader? And Who do I respect? How can I demonstrate the Respect Driver and Attributes? In asking these questions you will be able to identify opportunities to be more effective and define your own path to achieve true respect status with those you lead and influence.

Driver: Supportive

ELEMENT	DRIVER	ATTRIBUTES
Admiration	Supportive	15 > Loyal 16 > Dependable 17 > Encouraging

A.R.T.ful Leaders are keenly aware of the primary responsibility to provide proactive support for their people. Leaders need to instill in their people a sense of openness so that they do not hesitate to come to the leader when they need assistance to *remove barriers* that stand in the way of success. If a leader does not create this sense of goodwill within their team, leadership support will be lacking. Barriers may come in many forms. Examples include resolving internal conflicts within a team or across teams, providing resources or accessing resources needed to move forward, negotiating for the team when their efforts have not been fruitful, or providing executive sponsorship needed to add credibility to an initiative. When individuals lack the assurance that their leader is willing and even anxious to support them, but rather have a sense that their leader is hesitant to support them, the leader will lack respect and be perceived as A.R.T.less.

A.R.T.less leaders who do not display Respect Drivers often don't support their team at all. They can be absent leaders who are too focused on managing up and politicizing to support their own team. They spend a great deal of time trying to make themselves look good rather than spending time making sure their team and function look good. If the same amount of time and energy were spent on leading and supporting the function and team, looking good would not be an issue.

Some A.R.T.less leaders spend time on command and control behaviors rather than supporting their teams. This is manifested in a leader whose directing is a one-way street. Often the leader who is overly controlling squanders the intellectual capital of their people and saps the energy from their organization. Neither approach is an effective method for fostering a supportive culture and being perceived with respect.

The key to providing leadership support is to determine what support looks like by those you lead and influence. This can be accomplished by asking, "What more can I do to help you be more effective?" The answer to this will determine what expectations your team has of you as a leader. Unfortunately, there are many leaders who never ask this question and therefore fall short in providing the support needed by their team.

Three attributes help describe the leader who displays the Supportive Driver. That leader is *loyal* to the individuals and team, is *dependable* in providing support, and provides *encouragement.*

Attribute 15 > Loyal

Loyalty is the outcome of fulfilling commitments that you have made to support the efforts of those you lead. Loyalty is providing support without waivering or hesitating. Commitments are actions that others need from you as a leader to ensure success. Support is defined not by you the leader but by those who need your support.

Loyalty is also demonstrated by your character. *In everything you do and in everything you say* you need to be perceived as being loyal to your team and the various stakeholders you serve. If you are perceived as self-serving and self-involved, your loyalty will be suspect.

Questions to ask to assess your loyalty attribute include the following:

- Do I know what support is needed within my organization?
- Do I make commitments to people to remove barriers that block their success?
- Do I follow through on my commitments?
- Do I come to my team's defense and support them as needed during challenging situations (when times get tough)?

How those you lead answer these question will determine the degree to which you are perceived as a loyal leader and determine your loyalty quotient.

Attribute 16 > Dependable

There are two key factors that distinguish dependable leaders: providing *consistent support* to your organization and demonstrating a *positive leadership presence.*

Consistent Support: Dependability is achieved when a leader provides consistent support. This is a dedication to ensuring that when your team or stakeholders need you they can depend on you to be there. It isn't about when you have time or when you can fit it in or when you are available to be bothered. It is about attending to the needs of the individuals you lead when needed. When you communicate and demonstrate that you are dedicated to providing support to ensure success this is understood, appreciated, and boosts your credibility as a leader. Your dedication to providing support needs to be continuously communicated and reinforced (acted upon). The result of your diligence will be rewarded by being viewed as a leader who is dependable, reliable, and a valuable success resource throughout the organization. Assess your level of dependability by asking the following questions:

- Do I deliver support consistently?
- When someone raises their hand, do I make myself available?
- When the pressure is on, do I rise to the challenge and take the heat; or do I look for "sacrificial lambs"?

The answers to these questions will determine whether or not you are viewed as a dependable leader.

Leadership Presence: The Dependable Leader is also one who displays a positive pattern of behavior. Demonstrating positive leadership style means "showing up" day in and day out, presenting yourself in a positive manner. In A.R.T.ful Leadership terms, your positive leadership means that (1) those you lead know what to expect from you, (2) you exhibit a consistent temperament, and (3) you communicate effectively through "communicating forward."

When you display *positive leadership in a consistent way*, people will want to interact with you. They will learn how best to approach you and will be at ease in interacting with you. In other words, through your actions, interactions, and communication, individuals know that when they interact with you, the exchange will be positive (even though the topic of the interaction may be challenging).

It is important that your leadership exhibit *consistent and respectful temperament.* A Respected leader must be able to control emotions, particularly negative emotions. A temperamental leader is one who is perceived as being moody, irrational, easily annoyed, or angered; and therefore one who should be avoided. A positive leadership presence requires a leader to be calm under pressure, steadfast in facing challenges, and resolved in leading the team through adversity. This is accomplished both through having a keen sense of self and a mastery of both nonverbal and verbal communication.

Finally, *communicating forward* means using communication to drive conversations and issues forward on a continuous basis. It is using proactive language instead of evaluative language. Communicating forward keeps lines of communication open and people engaged in the conversation. It encourages people to consider possibilities. Communicating forward is future focused, while communicating backwards focuses on the past (focusing on the problems rather than possibilities).

Leaders who have a tendency to communicate backwards use "evaluative speak," which focuses on finding fault, setting blame, and looking for problems rather than seeking solutions. Communicating forward is "can do" speak; communicating backwards is "can't do" speak.

Questions to ask to assess your leadership presence include:

- Am I consistent in providing support to everyone within my organization? Or am I perceived as providing no support or sporadic support by those I lead?
- Do I consistently present a positive temperament when interacting with those I lead? Do I let my emotions impact my interactions negatively? Can the people I lead determine my mood based on how things are going inside my organization?
- Do I have a clear sense that the individuals I lead are at ease when approaching me and communicate freely no matter what the topic?
- Am I deliberate in using language that encourages open discussions focused on possibilities and opportunities?

People desire consistency and dependability in their leaders. This requires a leader to exhibit a leadership presence that will earn the respect of those you lead and influence through a consistent set of supportive actions and behaviors.

"What's the Forecast?"
A Story of a Lack of Leadership Presence

My executive leader is a tyrant. The entire group is terrified of him. He screams, yells, belittles us, and calls us names. You name it; he does it. This behavior escalates if there is an issue with any of the projects that any of his team is in charge of. Any little thing will set him off. If we need his support, forget it; none of us dare even approach him to help out, because we will be criticized for not being able to handle it ourselves, and we will be accused of mismanagement or ineptitude. What we have learned is that mornings are the worst time of day; avoid him at all cost in the A.M. Any little thing will set him off in the morning. It is absolutely exhausting.

Two of us have gone to human resources and have filed complaints, but it seems they are slow to act. Out of the eight senior project managers, six of us are seeking transfers. Thank goodness we support one another, both on project work and emotionally.

My team has devised a way to secretly communicate our executive leader's mood on a daily basis by putting out a daily "mood forecast." Here is how it works. Whoever is unfortunate enough to make first contact with him is to broadcast the daily "mood forecast" to the rest of the team via email. This way we all know how unpleasant the day may become and how active we should be in avoiding him. All that is needed is to put one word in the "subject line" in the email and send it off. Here is the forecast map:

Hurricane—Avoid him at all costs; he is in a foul mood. If you see him, run.

Cloudy—Grumpy and moody. Avoid if possible.

Sunny—Actually pleasant. If you need anything, today is the day! This happens as often as the sun shines in Seattle.

Attribute 17 > Encouraging

In my experience working as a consultant and coach to countless leaders and teams through the years, it is clear that a leader must provide supportive encouragement for a High Performing Team to be realized. A leader provides supportive encouragement by possessing a deep understanding of what is happening in the organization, keeping lines of communication open, staying engaged with the team, and setting the tone within the organization by remaining positive.

Organizational Understanding: An A.R.T.ful Leader displays strong organizational understanding. The leader needs to be constantly aware of what concerns the people he or she is leading may have. What are people discussing in the lunch room, around the water cooler, in the "meetings after the meetings," and in one another's offices? Those issues may potentially sap the energy out of the organization and keep individuals from being productive. If you either do not know what these issues are, or know what the issues are and ignore them, it will be impossible for you to provide the level of support needed to move your organization forward. In fact, if you are not engaged you will likely be viewed as being the main cause of the problem rather than the solution to the problem. A supportive leader understands the issues and takes the initiative to address the issues that are blocking productivity.

"Unaware"

A Story of a Lack of Organizational Understanding

I was working with an organization that was facing low employee satisfaction. I asked the leaders what was "top of mind" for the employees that could potentially be causing the current situation. The leaders didn't really know. They blamed a couple of the employees for being negative, and they admitted to knowing that there was a lot of talk and whispering going on in the office but didn't know what people were talking about.

So I went after the information myself. What I discovered from the employees is that the majority had a complete lack of respect for leadership. They explained that leadership was completely out of touch with what was going on in the organization. They didn't understand the issues that each of them faced to get things done, the problems that they were having in executing, and on and on and on. They said that when they tried to bring issues up to leadership they were just shut down and basically told to "stop complaining and get back to work." This caused the employees to cease engaging with their leaders.

They also indicated that leadership was paranoid and didn't want them talking to one another. One employee said that she was leaving the office of another employee after meeting to discuss a project when a senior leader in the group stopped her and said, "What were you talking to her for?" The employee was caught completely off guard and felt that she was doing something wrong when, in fact, they were working on a project. It was this type of interaction that had completely destroyed the credibility of the leadership team. The leaders were out of touch and had blinders on regarding what was happening in their own organization.

Communicate: Once you understand what is going on inside your organization, step up and take action. Communicate your stance on issues and do it in a positive manner. Taking the lead on addressing issues of concern to the organization demonstrates supportive engagement. Communication must bring the entire organization together. Leaders who provide information and context to issues from the leadership perspective and show how leadership is concerned and committed to resolving issues will be much more likely to be viewed as supportive and gain respect. If you are a leader who conceals information you will likely force your team members to draw their own conclusions through your silence (in the lunchroom, in meetings after the meetings, and around the water cooler). An attitude of "ignore it and it will go away" is not an effective response, but sadly it is one I have observed many times.

The most effective communication approach is empathic communication, which can be accomplished by doing the following:
1. **Acknowledge the issue.**
2. **Communicate empathy.** Indicate that you are concerned about the issue and are determined to address the issue (this puts you on the same side as your team).
3. **Communicate the current state.** Provide clarification on the issue. Use caution here. Don't call out any inaccuracies that you have heard that are being circulated in the organization; this is not helpful. Stick with the facts. Always take the high-road and stay positive; "communicate forward."
4. **Set expectations.** Describe what you intend to do to address the issue(s). If the issue can be resolved, explain what actions will be taken. If

the issue can't be resolved, then state that reality and why that is the case; be as honest as you can. Finally, if it can't be resolved, spend time in discussing how the issue can be better handled to reduce the frustration your team is experiencing. Help them work through the issue. Make sure you indicate what you need from the team and what they can expect from you.

5. **Show appreciation.** Communicate your genuine appreciation for the work and value the team brings to the organization. Practice patience as you work through the issue(s) of concern.

Keeps engaged: As Ken Blanchard said, "Help people reach their full potential. Catch Them Doing Something Right."[1] Continuously provide encouragement. Look for opportunities to acknowledge contributions. Encouragement is not providing rewards. Encouragement is consistently and continuously acknowledging contributions and showing genuine appreciation. I truly believe this doesn't happen enough. If you think that you do this, are you sure? I believe you can't say "thank you" to your team enough. It makes a difference. Know what your people are doing and acknowledge their contributions. That is the essence of supportive encouragement. If you don't, you will lose respect.

After a presentation on A.R.T.ful Engagement, a leader came up to me to thank me, and we started to chat. He was telling me how difficult it was to practice what I was talking about in his organization's culture. I asked him why. He explained that he thought it really boiled down to the fact that the culture of the organization was extremely competitive and thankless (that is actually how he described it).

He went on to say that he was charged with trying to improve the culture but was struggling because people were resistant. I asked him to describe what resistance he was experiencing. He told me that recently he had been at an organizational event to celebrate the conclusion of a very visible initiative that had been successful. He had made sure to find the key individuals responsible for the initiative and thanked them for their hard work. He also made an effort to find the executive leader of the group. He told the executive leader what a terrific event it was and what a tremendous job the team had done in executing all the components of the initiative. He called out specific elements that each of the team members had accomplished that he thought were notable. The executive leader's reaction was, "That's their job!" He was taken aback at how the executive responded. He couldn't believe that the executive didn't take great pride in the team's accomplishments. He was certain that the executive did not acknowledge the team for their efforts.

I immediately understood what this individual meant by a "thankless" culture. I also understood how difficult it was going to be to begin to incorporate supportive encouragement into the fabric of leadership within the organization. A culture that is one of "what have you done for me lately" is sad indeed and lacks the essence of being supportive and respected. I wished him much success and expressed that from what he described it was very evident that the work he is doing is sorely needed by the organization.

Remain Positive: At the risk of overusing metaphors, let me say that a leader needs to be the best coach, the best cheerleader, and the best motivational speaker possible. You set the tone for the organization. Your people watch you constantly, and they will talk about everything you say and do. The imprint you leave with each interaction you have with those you lead will reflect how respected you are within the organization. As a leader you need to realize that you live in a fishbowl, like it or not.

Your responsibility is to remain positive and live with your "glass half-full" at all times. Quite frankly, this does impact leadership presence. This doesn't mean that you can't be realistic or be pragmatic in your approach or that you can't be serious or passionate as a leader. What it does mean is that you approach people and issues with a sense of positivity. When you approach things with a positive energy this will be noticed and others will be energized by you.

"All Smiles, No Substance"
A Story of a Lack of Genuine Positivity

My leader is positive ALL the time . . . chipper, happy, and upbeat. There is only one problem: I don't believe it for a minute. It just simply doesn't seem genuine. It seems fake. I appreciate the effort, but the result simply falls flat. It is a joke around the office. He needs to realize it isn't about putting the smiley face on; it actually is about connecting with the team, and that doesn't happen. Everything is glossed over with that "everything is rosy" attitude. Everything is surface with him. It is like dealing with someone who is wearing a mask. Knock, knock, is anybody home?

Above all, this positivity must be genuine. Whatever "positive" looks like to you, do it and make sure it is real. If you can't be positive, figure it out because a leader who is a curmudgeon (love that word—look it up) simply saps the energy out of the team.

"Always There":
Story of a Supportive Leader

My leader is the most supportive leader that I have ever had the pleasure to work with. No matter how busy he is, I know that he will make time for me. No matter what he is doing he will always get back to me. With both our extremely busy schedules, we may not see one another face-to-face for a couple of weeks at a time. However, he protects our bi-weekly one-on-one meetings. He has made it a top priority to ensure that we stay connected.

During the times that we are not in contact he will either drop by the office just to say "hi" or will send me a quick email to "check in" to see if there is anything I need from him. He never passes up an opportunity to express his appreciation for me and my team.

I respect him tremendously for his resiliency and sprit. He has a way of looking for possibilities—always. When I am faced with a crisis and am a bit disillusioned or running on empty he has a way to make me think differently about things. He focuses on the positive and on resolutions and doesn't allow me to focus on problems. Because of our leader's support and positive approach there is just a continuous sense of forward motion in our group. Everyone feels it.

Driver: Demonstrate Mutual Respect

ELEMENT	DRIVER	ATTRIBUTES
Admiration	Demonstrate Mutual Respect	18 > Respectful 19 > Approachable 20 > Genuine Interest in Others

Mutual Respect is mentioned most often as a key driver to being perceived as a respected leader in our research. Mutual Respect exists when both parties respect one another as equals. Truly A.R.T.ful Leaders fundamentally understand that they can only achieve being perceived with Mutual Respect by treating the individuals they lead as equals. In my experience, this is a tall order for leaders who covet their titles more then they appreciate their responsibility as a leader and appreciate the contributions of each member of their team.

A.R.T.ful Leaders understand that treating others respectfully as equals actually unleashes human potential. A.R.T.ful Leaders who practice Mutual Respect acknowledge the contribution each member of the team brings to the table. This is obvious, right? Wrong. Unfortunately there are leaders who suffer from what I call Leadership Arrogance. If you don't have the same title as them, then you are less than them or not as important or not as valued. I have run into Leadership Arrogance in my consulting work and have heard countless stories of this disrespectful behavior. Here is one of them.

> While working on cultural transformation with a client it became clear that one barrier to a vibrant culture was Leadership Arrogance. Because of this, the company lacked open communication and engagement, and was not collaborative. In addition, or as a result (which came first, the chicken or the egg?), there was a vast trust void throughout the ranks. All, by the way, were desired cultural values. So what was the root cause of the company's issues? It seemed there was an unwritten norm within the company that employees were only allowed to talk to individuals who were one level higher then themselves on the organizational hierarchy, and no higher. As hard to believe as this might be, this was the norm. Now, you wouldn't find this in the employee handbook, but it was a widely-held norm within the organization. If you were to break this rule, you would be met with silence at the least, harshly criticized, and in certain instances your manager would be informed to have a chat with you so this behavior would cease.

The three attributes of Mutual Respect are for a leader to be *respectful of all*, *approachable*, and *show genuine interest* in each individual they lead.

Attribute 18 > Respectful

Leaders need to live by the Golden Rule: Do unto others as you would have them do unto you. Be respectful to each person inside and outside the organization.

Respect is reciprocal. Leaders can expect that their title will be received with a certain level of respect, but respect for your leadership is something that is earned. Show respect and it will be returned; don't and it won't. Act with leadership arrogance and suffer the consequences.

Respect is exhibited in a variety of ways: being cordial, showing interest, extending yourself, showing empathy, making eye contact when speaking to people, actually listening (instead of talking), asking questions, mirroring language used by those you are speaking to, and in many other ways. When you treat others as equal to you as a leader it will be noticed. Respectful behaviors will be appreciated. Respectful behaviors will be returned.

Attribute 19 > Approachable

Being approachable is actually a bi-product of being respectful. In other words, when you demonstrate respect you are perceived as being approachable. If you are not respectful, it is unlikely that you will be perceived as approachable.

Whether a leader is approachable or not is dependent on being open and engaging. Leaders need to take the initiative to engage to be perceived as approachable. The leader sets the tone.

Seek opportunities to engage in simple conversations with those you lead. Those simple conversations begin to create open lines of communication. In addition, live curious: engage your team and find out how things are going and what they are working on from time to time. A leader should not need a reason to talk to his or her team.

Engaging your staff begins to create a community. I know many organizations that have "Open Door Policies" but have few leaders within the organization who actually live the policy. Again, leaders set the tone. It is remarkable what a truly approachable leader is able to discover by creating open channels of communication within their team.

Questions to assess your level of approachability (your approachability quotient):

- Am I diligent about looking for opportunities to have conversations with my team (however brief)?
- Do I look for ways to engage my staff in conversations on various topics that may be of interest to them?
- Do I make sure that I make eye contact with my staff members when I walk through the office?
- Do I make it a point to greet my staff when walking through the office?
- Do I really attempt to live curious when interacting with my staff?

Attribute 20 > Genuine Interest in Others

Respected leaders who practice mutual respect show *genuine interest* every time they have an opportunity to interact with team members. Leaders need to take a true and genuine interest in what their team has to offer and contribute to the organization. It is so important that you create an environment in which every team member feels valued. You need to establish a culture of invitation where team members know they can bring ideas or suggestions forward, and they will be heard and considered because their contributions are valued and their perspectives are important. This sense of genuine interest is an important component to creating a vibrant and engaged team. Again, live curious as a leader and seek contributions from everyone (avoid the perception of being the smartest person in the room). Innovation and creativity depends on ideas and contributions and perspectives proposed through diversity of thought. This is at the heart of a leader who is genuinely interested in the people they lead and influence.

Driver: Responsible and Accountable

ELEMENT	DRIVER	ATTRIBUTES
Admiration	Responsible and Accountable	21 > Responsible for Own Actions, 22 > Sets Expectations 23 > Holds People Accountable

If there is a hot button in organizations it tends to be around the notion of accountability—who is and who isn't held accountable. What is accountability, and what does it mean within an organization? Many organizations put much time and energy in making sure that accountabilities are recorded in systems and then don't do anything with them. Despite this, being responsible and accountable is a key driver for a leader to earn the respect of those they lead.

The key attributes of being a Responsible and Accountable leader are: *being responsible for your own actions* first, *setting expectations* of others and once set, actually *holding people accountable.*

Attribute 21 > Responsible for Own Actions

Leaders must be accountable for their own actions to be perceived with respect. Leaders not responsible for their own actions will fall short in being viewed as A.R.T.ful. If you are unable to hold yourself accountable you will lack the credibility to hold those you lead accountable.

Leaders need to set accountabilities for themselves. This will set the standards of accountablity for the rest of the organization. It should be clear to your team what you are directly accountable and responsible for as the leader. This sets expectations of what your team can expect from you. If I were to ask you, "What specifically are you accountable and responsible for as a leader?" what would your answer be? More importantly, if I asked your team members the same question, what would their answer be? Would their answer reflect your answer? If they can't answer the questions then they are unclear what contributions you actually make as a leader of the organization. If your answer and their answer are not the same, then you have a fundamental alignment issue that needs to be resolved.

There is nothing more frustrating for a team then to perceive a leader as being accountable for absolutely nothing. If that is the perception, then the team concludes that you are in the position to do the following: *take credit* for everything that goes well in your organization and *deflect* anything that doesn't go right in your organization to someone else. When leadership lacks accountability, it breeds a culture where individuals are always on the defensive.

A.R.T.ful Leadership includes the ability to be clear on what you are accountable for as the leader. It is also being ultimately responsible for the results of your organization. A respected leader is one who shares responsibility for the organization's successes as well as the organization's shortcomings. A respected leader steps up in times when individuals or teams fall short and asks, "What is my contribution to this, and what is my obligation as the leader to improve this going forward?" When leaders share responsibility for organizational shortcomings and actively partner to turn things around, using missteps as a learning opportunity, they earn a great deal of respect by those they lead.

"I Haven't a Clue"
A Story of an Unaccountable Leader

My senior leader is apparently not responsible or accountable for anything that happens in the function. I haven't a clue what her job is. I know I report to her, but I don't know what her job is beyond that. I have asked, but she doesn't answer. I know I have to hand in my weekly reports to her, and I know she bundles them together along with my peers and passes them along. But besides that, I haven't a clue what she actually does to contribute to achieving organizational goals. I have no idea what she works on, if anything. If it is sending out emails and agendas and gathering reports from me and peers, that doesn't seem to be enough to be a senior leader. I don't find her credible at any level. I am simply baffled.

Attribute 22 > Sets Expectations

Leaders must set clear expectations on what they expect individuals and teams to deliver. Individuals desire that their leader establish clear expectations. Leaders who do not set expectations are expecting their people to operate in a performance void. What will be good enough? What will be criticized? What will be rewarded? Without clear expectations individuals simply don't know what to expect.

Setting expectations requires the following elements:

1. **Determine the *What*:** Define what the deliverables are. Be specific on what you expect to be produced or delivered.
2. **Identify the *When*:** Be sure individuals know when each deliverable is due. Again, be specific.
3. **Include *Measurement*:** Clearly define the measure(s) that will be used to measure success. Measurement can be in dollars, various quality measures, customer satisfaction, or a variety of other measures. Key is that you define what "good" looks like. Set the criteria for how each expectation will be evaluated.

Again, it is clear through our research that individuals want to know what is expected of them. Set clear expectations, communicate the expectations, and ensure that the expectations are understood. Finally, make sure that you communicate your involvement, if any, in achieving each of the expectations you set for your team.

"Bait and Switch"
Story of a Leader Not Setting Expectations

My leader doesn't set expectations for any of my team members. It is frustrating. His answer to that is: "Do what is necessary to satisfy the customer." So that is what we do. Then when we do that, our leader turns around and finds fault either with what we did or finds ways to criticize us for the outcome that was achieved. Everything we do is just not good enough. We have tried and tried to have discussions as individual team members and as a team to have our leader define expectations for our group. It just doesn't happen. It is a bait and switch tactic to keep us from being rewarded for our work. If you don't have set expectations, then guess what, there is no way you can ever actually meet them! It is hugely frustrating and a complete waste of time.

Attribute 23 > Holds People Accountable

Once you have set expectations it is critical to hold people accountable. Organizational members want leaders to hold people accountable, consistently accountable, across the organization. Repeatedly in our studies, holding people accountable is tied to a leader being respected as a leader. Consistency is the key factor for a leader to be perceived with respect when managing performance. If a leader is not consistent in holding people accountable, respect will suffer.

Leaders have to be diligent in holding everyone to the same performance standards (this begins with setting consistent expectations across the organization). It is extremely irritating when organizational members view certain team members as "skating by" or being held to a different level of performance when it comes to contributing to the organization. It even becomes more irritating when they perceive their leader as not holding these individuals accountable for subpar performance, particularly if they believe that when it comes to their own performance they are held to very high standards. Leaders must understand that this is noticed, discussed among the team members, and negatively impacts the leader's credibility.

Accountability is all about a leader's ability to manage performance. Performance management is a skill that at times is unpleasant but must be mastered by every leader. What I have noticed in my work with managers and those in "leadership" positions (typically those with a "director" title or above in most organizations) is this: managers quite often are better at managing performance than their leadership counterparts. I attribute this to managers having their primary focus in managing people, whereas those in leadership positions are primarily focused on managing processes and functional issues rather than people.

Therefore, I am the first to recognize that managers are often the most A.R.T.ful Leaders in organizations when it comes to performance management. However, leaders are not immune to the necessity to manage performance and must be diligent in holding people accountable. As you climb the ranks within an organization, individuals tend to be more critical of your ability to manage performance and hold people accountable, so be diligent because it will impact your ability to be perceived with respect.

Driver: Provides Feedback and Counsel

ELEMENT	DRIVER	ATTRIBUTES
Respect	Provides Feedback and Counsel	24 > Seeks Feedback 25 > Provides Feedback

I want to begin by telling a story, and for this I am drawing from my own experience.

"All Feedback has Value"
A Story of the Value of Feedback

I was discussing the importance of feedback several years ago with Michael Howe who was the CEO of MinuteClinic at the time. It was a lively discussion. We both are passionate about the value of feedback. During the conversation Michael shared with me his view on the importance of feedback by stating the following (and I am paraphrasing):

There is value in all feedback, even feedback that you don't agree with. Because when you don't agree with feedback it reveals important information. What it reveals is that the person delivering the feedback doesn't know what they are talking about. The key then is to determine how the person can be so incorrect in their perception of you. That is really powerful information to consider, because you have to start with that perception in order to begin to change things going forward. The focus has to be on doing things differently so the person giving you the feedback views you more accurately going forward.

Michael's point of view provided me with a fresh lens in looking at feedback. We discussed how challenging it is to get people to view feedback as a powerful tool, particularly when people deliver it poorly, don't have an accurate picture at times when they deliver the feedback, or often offer uninvited feedback. We also strategized how MinuteClinic could create a feedback culture, and what the responsibility of leadership and of each employee is in a feedback culture. That discussion and the subsequent work that was done was incredibly successful. Under Michael's leadership a feedback culture was created and was sustained until his departure. Our work is a case study for how to build a feedback culture within an organization.

As a leader, you have the opportunity to leave a positive imprint on your organization and the individuals you lead by creating a feedback culture. A **feedback culture** *is one where feedback is desired and actively sought by members within your organization.* This can only be achieved when feedback is viewed as a positive source of information for individuals and teams to be more effective. Unfortunately this is often not the case for the following reasons:

- **Feedback is delivered in the wrong context.** Feedback is information. When someone provides feedback, they are offering information. In addition, feedback is offering advice or suggesting actions. The person receiving the feedback can then consider incorporating the suggestions to increase effectiveness moving forward. If feedback is delivered as a means to correct action, to direct (or demand) someone to do something, or to reprimand someone for something they have done, this is not feedback. It is actually managing performance. All of these are forms of "telling" behaviors or "directive" communication. Directive communication doesn't allow choice. Don't confuse "telling" with feedback.

- **Feedback is not delivered with a consultative approach.** Feedback is consultative in nature, because it provides a choice to the person that is receiving the feedback. Feedback must be delivered in the spirit of providing information, advice, wisdom, and suggestions to someone in order for them to be more effective. The person receiving feedback has the choice to act on the information or not to act. If you don't deliver feedback in this consultative context, you will be frustrated with the results of your efforts when your feedback is ignored. If you need to direct instead of provide feedback, then do that from the start. If you are managing performance or holding someone accountable, then don't disguise it as providing feedback. When you do so, it tarnishes the true nature of feedback and negatively impacts your credibility as a leader.
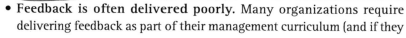

- **Feedback is often delivered poorly.** Many organizations require delivering feedback as part of their management curriculum (and if they don't, they should). Unfortunately, much of the training actually teaches leaders how to deliver feedback in the context of managing performance (performance reviews, corrective action, developing people) and NOT in the true spirit of delivering feedback. Therefore, managers learn how to deliver feedback by "telling" or using directive communication rather than delivering feedback in using a consultative approach.

- **Feedback is often delivered irregularly.** Most organizations provide little to no feedback to one another. In a study we conducted relating to feedback, 80% responded that they only received feedback during performance reviews, and 90% of the respondents indicated that they desired more feedback. Feedback needs to occur more frequently. It needs to be part of the very fabric of the organization. Once it becomes ingrained as part of the organization it becomes a pattern of conversation rather than a special type of conversation. Infrequent feedback feels stilted, unnatural, and awkward for everyone involved. It doesn't have to be that way, and it shouldn't be.

- **Feedback is owned by the wrong person.** In the majority of organizations feedback is owned by the person delivering feedback (which in most cases is the leader). That is the wrong approach. The person owning feedback should be the person seeking feedback, not the person delivering feedback. The person delivering feedback has no obligation to change behavior. The ownership of feedback in organizations is simply upside down. The only way to correct this is to create a feedback culture where feedback is desired, expected, and sought. When this is the case, people will become responsible for their own feedback. When individuals become responsible for their own feedback and actively seek feedback they will begin to own the feedback they receive and act upon the feedback.

- **People have not been taught how to receive feedback.** Organizations may spend time training how to give feedback, but virtually none train individuals on how to receive feedback. In fact, receiving feedback is not part of any curriculum (unless you happen to major in communications and happen to have the right curriculum). When I have controlled an organization's curriculum I have made "receiving feedback" mandatory for all employees; it is that important. Not only do you as leader need to know how to receive feedback, you need to teach your people how to receive feedback and continuously reinforce how to receive feedback appropriately. During my coaching sessions I review the guidelines of receiving feedback during the start of each coaching session. This places the person receiving feedback in the right frame of mind to be more receptive when being offered information and recommendations that will assist in making them more effective.

Keys to Building a Feedback Culture

Establishing a feedback culture takes focus, commitment, and dedication by leadership. It begins by fostering a view of feedback being a key to success. Feedback cultures view feedback in the following ways:

1. Feedback is information.
2. All feedback is valuable.
3. Never reject feedback—no matter who it is coming from.
4. The goal in feedback is to "seek to understand."
5. If the feedback is inaccurate ask yourself the following questions:
   "What is my contribution to this misperception?"
   "What is my obligation moving forward to change the perception for the better?"

As a leader you can begin to create your own feedback culture by viewing feedback in the ways described above. If you take that step, be careful: you need to "walk the talk."

Attribute 24 > Seeks Feedback

Often leaders struggle with this attribute. Leaders shouldn't need feedback, since they should have all the answers, right? Actually, no. Leaders need feedback in order to gauge how they are being perceived by the organization and to determine what their team needs from them to be successful.

When seeking feedback, the key is for a leader to ask for feedback in the right way. Let's face it, if a leader walks up to someone who reports to them and asks, "How am I doing?" or "Give me some feedback," it is likely that what they will hear is what the person thinks they want to hear rather than the truth (that is, if the person is wise). This type of feedback does nothing to help your leadership capability. It may be helpful in stroking your ego, but it is not meaningful in actually helping you be a more effective leader.

So how should a leader ask for feedback? Here is the advice that I have given to leaders at all levels to glean meaningful information from individuals they lead. Ask for feedback in a way that asks for feedback based on the individual's perspective. Consider the difference in the following:

Not effective: "Alex, tell me what I can do to be more effective?"

If Alex reports to you, you have just asked Alex for evaluative feedback. Alex is not likely to evaluate your leadership. Alex will scramble to appease you instead of telling you the truth.

> *Effective:* "Alex, what can I do to help you be more effective?" or "Alex, what can I do to be more supportive in helping you achieve your goals?"

Requesting feedback in this way allows Alex to provide you feedback in the context of what you can do to help him rather than asking him to evaluate you. There is a distinct difference. This is a much more effective way to seek honest information from Alex. When Alex answers the question, you need to be able to receive the feedback.

Receiving Feedback

"No one can make you feel inferior without your permission."
Eleanor Roosevelt

Leaders need to seek feedback and actually receive feedback to be respected. When you emulate the proper method for receiving feedback you begin to set expectations for how everyone in the organization should behave when receiving feedback. As a leader, it is suggested that you follow these guidelines and use these within your own organization to create a positive culture for receiving feedback:

Guidelines for Receiving Feedback
1. **Listen** (wait).
2. **Keep neutral** (listen without emotion).
3. **Resist arguing or becoming defensive.**
4. **Ask questions.** Ask, ask, ask. Seek to understand. Ask questions to ensure you understand the feedback.
5. **Thank them. Thank the individual for their feedback.** You can thank someone for sharing information without agreeing with the feedback. If you don't agree with the feedback, information, or suggestions being offered, then merely thank them for their time. Above all, be appreciative and genuine.
6. **Take time to process the information. Give yourself a timeout.** Take time to process what you have heard. Even if the feedback was not delivered skillfully, or perhaps came from someone you do not perceive as A.R.T.ful. Remember, feedback is information and all information is valuable. Separate the person from the information.

7. Look into the mirror or through the eyes of the person giving you feedback. If you believe the feedback is inaccurate, answer the following: "What is my contribution to this perception? and "What is my obligation going forward to change things?"

Attribute 25 > Provides Feedback

Leaders should seek every opportunity to provide feedback. When you have an opportunity to provide feedback, take it. Providing feedback in real-time is the best opportunity to provide relevant feedback and actually assist in helping people become more effective. Continuous feedback allows individuals to take small actions rather than the major behavioral changes that may be required when feedback is irregular.

The best analogy regarding continuous feedback is that of a football coach. I only am using a football coach, because I am a fanatical college football fan, so am speaking from experience. I always know when I am watching a well-coached team by whether or not the coach is giving feedback to the players. The best coaches provide immediate feedback throughout the game. The coach immediately acknowledges players for doing things well as they come off the field, and they immediately will pull a player aside and skillfully provide feedback when things don't go as planned. A leader should do the same.

What isn't effective is to wait to deliver feedback until the feedback is irrelevant, because it relates to behavior that has happened far in the past. When this type of feedback is given it always will be perceived as a reprimand rather than feedback from someone who really cares about them. I know as a parent I do not hesitate to provide my children with feedback if I believe that what I have to offer will assist them in becoming more effective in whatever they may be doing. I don't wait, and I don't hesitate. I deliver feedback immediately because I care deeply about their wellbeing. I try to lead the same way. To do anything less would be delivering feedback with an "I told you so" approach. That will never be perceived with credibility.

Seek every opportunity to acknowledge contributions as well, since it will motivate similar behavior. In addition, seek every opportunity to "coach" in real-time to guide individuals in the direction to be more effective, incrementally. The focus should be on providing continuous feedback. When you achieve this, you will undoubtedly diminish the need to worry about having to manage performance.

The following are guidelines for delivering feedback. Follow these guidelines when you have an opportunity to coach individuals and teams (and peers). These should be followed closely, and over time your skill in delivering feedback will increase. As your skill increases, you will find that individuals will begin to seek you out to provide them feedback. When this is the result you will know that you are perceived as a respected leader in providing feedback.

Guidelines for Delivering Feedback

1. Invite the individual to provide their own perspective first.
2. Ask questions to draw out relevant comments from the individual about their performance or objectives.
3. Focus on what actually happened based on observed performance (when possible). Explain in terms of where the performance currently is versus where the performance should be to be truly effective.
4. Discuss strengths, as well as areas where improvement is needed in order to increase effectiveness.
5. Avoid comparisons with other individuals.
6. Provide feedback that is clear, tactful, and constructive. Be conversational.
7. Encourage the individual to identify key areas which, if improved, will result in the greatest improvement.
8. Finish on a high note by acknowledging areas of achievement (acknowledge the individual's strengths).

Respect Driver: Fair and Balanced

ELEMENT	DRIVER	ATTRIBUTES
Respect	Fair and Balanced	26 > Provides Opportunities to All 27 > Rewards and Recognizes Consistently 28 > Resolves Issues Fairly

The final driver of Respect is to be fair and balanced when leading. Showing favoritism to a few will result in deep divides among individuals within your team and will potentially cause factions within the organization. If this happens, your organization will not function at a high level. As a leader you are responsible for creating and sustaining cohesiveness within your organization. This is not an easy task, since by nature individuals will create their own competitiveness from time to time. Also, conflicts between individuals will erupt; it is a natural part of people working together. During such times you will need to calm the waters so your team can remain focused on what is important to the organization and not expend energy on unproductive behavior. This requires you to be unbiased in *providing opportunities to all* within your organization, to *reward and recognize individuals* and teams with a high degree of consistency, and be fair and sensitive in *resolving issues.*

Attribute 26 > Provides Opportunities to All

Leaders are always balancing the pressures caused by changes in the internal and external environment. Internal pressures come from organizational expansions and/or contractions. External pressures come from constant pressures to meet changing customer demands and adapting in order to keep ahead of the competition. Responding to these seemingly unending changes can be exhausting for leaders, as well as team members. Even during times of "steady state," leaders find that organizations are always shuffling resources, restructuring or implementing initiatives, taking steps to streamline the organization, or are focusing on a whole host of other organizational imperatives.

Change breeds opportunities for leaders to manage change. During these times it is expected that a leader will utilize their strategic ability (one of the drivers of Admiration) to successfully navigate change as quickly as possible. As a leader, you must be cognizant when managing these opportunities that you are diligent in presenting opportunities fairly to your organizational members. This is a balancing act, but it is clear through our research that if you are not deliberate in providing opportunities fairly across the organization it will impact your credibility negatively. You can prevent being viewed as only providing opportunities to a few, or showing favoritism by doing the following:

> **Demonstrate objectivity**: As a leader be objective and inclusive when providing opportunities. Guard against being biased in deliberately presenting opportunities to only a few within your organization. If you only provide opportunities to a few, those not presented with opportunities will view you as showing favoritism. There are times when it is clear that there is a perfect individual within an organization for a particular role. You may also create a certain role specifically with a particular individual in mind, but these should be the exception and not the rule. The key is balance.

> Leaders need to be deliberate in managing opportunities. Look for opportunities that will stretch individuals within the organization and thereby increase your organizations capacity. The following are ways to guard against being viewed as playing favorites:

- Offering assignments and projects as a means to spread opportunities across the organization.
- Allowing individuals to be considered for opportunities whenever possible.

If you don't you will lose credibility, lose respect, and lose talent.

Aggressively guard against allowing the perceptions of others to influence objectively: Remain objective in providing opportunities and selecting individuals for opportunities. Ensure that you are not influenced to provide opportunities to a select few or to block certain individuals from consideration. If you do this it will be noticed. If you are not objective you will create divisions in the ranks, which will cause disruption in productivity.

Communicate Opportunities: Communicate, communicate, communicate. Communicate what opportunities are available and how you intend to manage the opportunities. Once you have filled an opportunity, communicate that decision. Express your gratitude for individuals who showed interest in the opportunities. Always show gratitude in order to keep them engaged and interested in future opportunities.

"Disrespected and Demoralized"
A Story of Not Providing Opportunities to All

I guess I should consider myself lucky to be part of a growing organization, but I don't. It would appear that we are expanding, but the opportunities that are coming online are only available for those who are our senior leader's favorites. If you play his game and don't cause any friction and are a "kiss up," you get ahead. If you don't, you are out. I am apparently out. I wouldn't consider myself a trouble-maker—far from it. I work hard, really hard. I consistently over-deliver and am highly respected by key influencers and executives throughout the organization. Unfortunately, my senior leader isn't one of them. I guess I don't play the game or spend enough time stroking his ego. I don't have the time, and it just isn't in me to do that. If I can't be rewarded for what I deliver, then I guess this isn't the place for me.

I was asked to meet with my senior leader. He explained how terrific the organization is doing and how great I have been doing (he never does that, so I knew something was up). He then explained in cryptic language that new opportunities were going to be created. He then told me which opportunity that I would be taking; yes, taking. I wasn't told what other opportunities were being created, just the one that I was being moved into. I asked, but he wouldn't tell me about any other opportunities. The opportunity that I was being placed into had less scope, less authority, less organizational impact, and doesn't utilize my skills. I explained this to him in very nice terms. It didn't matter; it had already been decided.

A few days later I begin to hear that my peers who don't perform at the same level as me (I believe this to be true and many within my function believe this to be true as well) started to receive promotions in newly created positions. I didn't know these positions were going to become available and did not have an opportunity to discuss these opportunities. The individuals who were given these positions are widely considered the senior leader's favorites within our division. I get that this happens from time to time, but every single position was given to a select few—and this has become a pattern. As a result, I am completely demoralized about not being recognized for my dedication and contributions made to this organization the past several years. I don't see any future for me here. None.

Attribute 27 > Rewards and Recognizes Consistently

Being perceived as fair and consistent reflects in how leaders reward and recognize their team. Rewards are noticed because of the financial impact they have on individuals. Although rewards are to be kept highly confidential, it is amazing how often this information is actually shared among team members. When word gets out that rewards have been distributed unequally or arbitrarily, it can ruin credibility. Leaders need to be resolute in fairly distributing rewards within the organization. Rewards must be distributed objectively, fairly, and without bias—and based on measures.

Similarly, don't make the mistake of NOT rewarding individuals for contributions in order to treat everyone the same. This is just as bad. This mistake often happens during annual salary reviews when leaders have to manage a percentage increase across their entire organization. Instead of determining who has contributed the greatest and rewarding individuals accordingly, leaders will just give everyone a marginal increase in an effort to treat everyone equally. To make matters worse, leaders actually tell individuals what they are doing, as if this is going to play well with the overachievers. This across-the-board approach is wrong, because individuals simply do not contribute to the organization at the same level. Leaders need to have the courage to make the tough decisions and do what is necessary to reward according to an individual's contribution. If this means that certain individuals may not get any increase so that those who have contributed greatly to the organization can be rewarded, then so be it. Rewarding fairly does not mean equally.

Leaders need to recognize everyone for their contributions. Not just the few, not just the ones who are the most visible, but everyone who has contributed to the organization's success. Many times I have heard stories about leaders who have publicly recognized managers for a major contribution and failed to recognize the front-line employees who actually did the work. Failing to properly recognize individuals for their achievements disenfranchises them and results in employees becoming disengaged and losing respect for leadership.

"Am I Invisible?"
A Story of Not Being Recognized

I must be invisible. Every time our leader recognizes our team for something the only one mentioned is our direct manager. No mention of the team. The leader goes on and on and on about how great a job our manager has done. It is nice that our leader acknowledges all the hard work. What is ridiculous is that our leader isn't acknowledging the people who actually do the work. What is worse, is that our manager doesn't say anything either; he just drinks it all in and takes all the accolades for himself. I quite frankly don't know how he can sleep at night. I try and do damage control with my team, but they are getting annoyed. This behavior happens in quarterly team meetings and in emails that are sent out by both our leader and direct manager. I have discussed this with my manager, but he just passes it off. I guess when you are invisible it just doesn't matter.

"Appreciated"
A Story of Being Recognized

My leader is terrific at always showing great appreciation for my contribution and the contributions of the team. At each one-on-one I have with him he looks for ways to recognize my achievements. This constant feedback and recognition is extremely gratifying and keeps me motivated. During team meetings he does the same thing; he looks for areas that he can recognize team achievements. When individuals within the team perform outstanding work he makes sure he communicates that achievement to executive leadership. We know that what we do, how we contribute, and all our hard work will not go unnoticed.

Attribute 28 > Resolves Issues Fairly

As a leader you will face resolving issues that arise within your organization. The quicker you respond the better. The longer you ignore issues and allow them to escalate into full-fledged conflicts the harder they are to manage. An A.R.T.ful Leader who earns respect keeps a close eye on issues that arise within their function (between individuals and between teams). They do this by keeping lines of communication open so that they are aware of potential issues that may be brewing within the organization. A.R.T.ful Leaders also develop keen insight on when their involvement is necessary to resolve issues. Finally, A.R.T.ful Leaders take action by using measured diplomacy and influence to resolve issues and stabilize the organization.

The key attribute in resolving issues is for a leader to take time to gather all information needed to appropriately respond to situations. To earn respect it is essential that you do not take sides when resolving issues within your organization. Take the time necessary to ensure that you respond by representing everyone involved. If you don't, your actions may actually escalate the issue rather than resolve the issue.

A leader who is reactive to issues without taking the time to gather all the facts will not be effective. A leader must investigate fully and consider various perspectives. The leader's responsibility is to be the voice of reason when attempting to bring competing sides together. A leader using fact finding, problem-solving skills, and reasoning will be much more successful than a leader who simply acts on limited information. If you respond in haste, you will likely miss key information that is critical to reach a resolution that is satisfactory for all involved and to be perceived as being fair.

Demonstrating Respect requires you to be a supportive leader, to be a leader who leverages the contributions of every member of the organization, no matter what level; who holds yourself and others accountable; builds a vibrant feedback culture; and is consistent and fair in providing opportunities, rewards, and recognition. These attributes contribute to your ability to be perceived as an A.R.T.ful Leader.

A.R.T.ful Leadership Reflection Journal

1. What leader have you Respected and why? What have you learned from their leadership that you can incorporate in your own leadership journey?

2. Which of the Respect Drivers (and Attributes) do you need to strengthen?

3. Who Respects you as a leader?

4. Who is critical for your success as a leader but may not Respect you? Why? What steps can you take to begin to change that perception?

6

Trust

A person who trusts no one can't be trusted.
Jerome Blatner

A man who doesn't trust himself can never truly trust anyone else.
Cardinal de Retz, *Memoires*

Trust men and they will be true to you; treat them greatly, and they will show themselves great.
Ralph Waldo Emerson

Trust: The ability of a leader to build trusting relationships with those they lead. This is initiated by extending trust to others. Trust increases through building and maintaining relationships.

I have had the opportunity to work with sales professionals in a variety of industries and countries throughout my career. When I begin working with a sales organization I typically observe two groups: I observe the top sales producers and the bottom producers. I do this to determine what behaviors successful top sales people exhibit that set them apart. What I have concluded time and again, particularly working with Adaytum Software (now Cognos) sales staff and global business partners, is that the most successful sales professionals do the following things extremely well:
  • **They have a unique ability to connect with people.** They make people feel comfortable and quickly cultivate relationships.

103

- **They are able to establish trust with individuals.** This is done by projecting themselves as open and honest. It also is a product of conveying a real interest in people. Finally, trust is established through projecting that they are truly committed to making a positive impact for the prospect (personalizing the sale).
- **They are expert communicators.** They listen really well (the poorest performers talk really well, but don't listen very well). They have a unique ability to use adaptive communication in order to make individuals comfortable in opening up and sharing information.

These are the characteristics that separate top performers from the rest of the pack. It isn't product knowledge, it isn't qualifying a sale, and it isn't the ability to negotiate that will close a sale. It is the ability to *connect with people*, *establish trust*, and *communicate* that will lead to peak performance.

As I started to work with leaders I made the same observations. The leaders who were able to create and sustain true and committed followership (A.R.T.ful Leaders) connect with people, are trusted, and establish open lines of communication. They have the same characteristics as the top performers in sales.

As I began to identify the Drivers and Attributes of A.R.T.ful Leadership it became clear that these three characteristics were linked to the A.R.T.ful Leadership element of Trust. It is through the building of trust that a leader is perceived as someone who is able to establish meaningful relationships with people, and is not simply the person who happens to be "the boss." If individuals trust a leader, they will follow that leader without hesitation. A leader establishes trust through creating open lines of communication. The characteristics that I observed in top sales professionals as well as in A.R.T.ful Leaders are infused throughout the Trust Drivers and Attributes.

TRUST DRIVERS

Note: *Skilled Communicator* is a key driver in establishing and sustaining Trust. It is through communication that leaders demonstrate the Drivers of Trust (and associated Attributes). Skilled Communicator will be infused throughout the discussion as a means to describe how communication is used to establish Trust as an A.R.T.ful Leader.

Trust Drivers: Definitions

The following are the five key Drivers for leaders to be Trusted by those they lead and influence:

Extends Trust: A trusted leader must extend trust and lead with trust. Demonstrating trust fosters trust in return.

Keeps Confidences: A trusted leader must demonstrate a high level of integrity in maintaining confidentiality. Individuals must know that when they provide information to a leader in confidence that the leader will keep that promise. If that promise is broken, information sharing will stop.

Honest: A trusted leader must demonstrate a high level of openness in discussions with those they lead and influence. This requires a leader to be straightforward in providing information that is critical to assist individuals to do their jobs or be successful. Information needs to be timely and needs to be delivered in the right medium to be appreciated.

Relationship Builder: A trusted leader has the ability to connect with individuals at a personal level that leads to open communications and strong bonds/commitment. Building strong interpersonal relationships aids in positively motivating and encouraging others.

Collaborative: A trusted leaser is able to share leadership in order to bring the best ideas and solutions to the forefront. This is also evident when a leader works tirelessly to create networks and partnerships both inside and outside the organization. When leaders are able to create and sustain strong connections and resource bonds they increase the perception of being a trusted advisor to those they lead and influence.

Trust Drivers: Key Attributes

Trust has been the issue of concern either directly are indirectly most often with my work with organizations over the years. The lack of trust breaks down communication, causes deep and widening problems between individuals, and over time erodes commitment and the desire for individuals to be part of the organization. I have found that when there is a trust issue within a function or team it often is systemic, meaning that it starts with the leader who has created a "trust void" within their organization, and this has bled throughout their team.

"Friday Is Too Close to Monday"
A Story of a Lack of Trust

I was discussing trust with a senior director ("Tom") a few weeks ago. Tom was expressing how disillusioned he was with the lack of trust that existed within his division and how difficult it was to continue to be engaged. I asked Tom what he attributed the trust void to within his organization. Without hesitating, he said it was his leader ("Kip") who had created the mistrust. I then asked Tom to describe what Kip had done to create the environment. Tom said that Kip lacked engagement. Tom said he seldom had any contact with Kip. There were few departmental team meetings. Team meetings were supposed to happen bi-weekly, but half of those were cancelled. In addition, Tom seldom met with Kip one-on-one because he showed little to no interest in meeting with him. If they did meet, perhaps once a month for half an hour, Kip would talk about other team members negatively, appear annoyed that he was being bothered, or would be negative in general about other parts of the organization. As a result, Tom had learned to share as little information as possible or to avoid Kip.

Tom also shared that Kip rarely responds to emails. Tom said he limits emails to Kip, because it just opens up an opportunity to get criticized. Still, there are times when he needs to provide Kip with updates, or ask Kip a question. When Tom sends a question to Kip that needs an answer, 80% of the time Kip does not reply, and if he does it becomes a quagmire of negativity. So once again, he had been conditioned to operate in a void.

Tom then said something that I found incredibly sad: he said that he was having a hard time coming to work each day. He said, "You know, it is funny how people get excited about Friday's. What I have realized is that I dread Fridays, because Friday is so close to Monday when I am going to have to start this whole thing over again." I encouraged him to focus on himself and to seek encouragement from A.R.T.ful relationships inside and outside the organization as a source of support. I also advised that it may be time to consider options in order to begin to enjoy Fridays once again and all the other days that lie ahead.

Much attention has been given to the topic of trust in leadership books over the past several years. Some approaches have associated all leadership skills to trust. Although useful, I find that some of these approaches lack focus. In developing the A.R.T.ful Leadership Model it was highly important to cast a magnifying glass on the most critical behaviors that are associated with a leader being perceived as a Trusted leader. In conducting surveys, interviews, and observing leaders it was critical to answer two questions:

"What do leaders do to gain trust?"

"What do leaders do to create trust voids within organizations?"

The answers to these two questions revealed the key Attributes leaders need to demonstrate in order to be perceived as trusted leaders.

Trust is a product of creating an open environment that sets the framework for dialogue between the leader and the individuals they lead. When a leader establishes an open environment this begins to be manifested across the team as team members interact with one another. This is not an easy task and is an intentional act on the part of leadership. I have worked with many leaders who struggle mightily to instill trust within their organizations due to their inability to exhibit trust. Clearly, leaders set the trust tone for the entire organization. The fact remains that if the leader does not trust their team, the team will not trust their leader.

The Nature of Trust

Trusting someone doesn't just happen. Trust is formed and therefore is experiential in nature. As a leader you need to understand the basic principles of human behavior when taking steps to gain trust.

First, *trust is incremental*. Trust is built over time. The majority of people just don't blindly trust others. People who tend to be "trusting" only need to be burned a couple of times to learn their lesson to be more cautious.

Survival instincts keep us on our guard and remind us that it isn't wise to trust without being somewhat cautious. As a leader you will be evaluated by those you lead over time to determine whether or not you can be trusted. Just because you hold a leadership role does not mean you automatically hold the trust card. Far from it.

Second, *trust is reciprocal.* It is unlikely for a person to extend trust to another person without being trusted in return. To do so would require someone to suspend sound judgment. Organizational members may act as though they trust you; after all, you are the leader. They may do this purely for political reasons (keep their job, move up the corporate ladder, be recognized, and so on). However, if they are not perceiving that you trust them, they will not extend trust to you in return.

Trust requires risk taking. Let's face it, trusting another person requires taking a risk that the person deserves your trust and will do right by you. When someone breaks trust it severely damages the relationship. This is true in both our personal lives and in our professional lives. Once trust is broken it is difficult to regain. Therefore, once trust is gained leaders must view this as a tremendous responsibility. Individuals are taking a risk by trusting you; don't let them down.

Who Trusts You as a Leader?

Trust is a key element of A.R.T.ful Leadership because of the benefits it provides to the organization, leader, and team. When I coach leaders around Trust I ask them, "Do your people trust you?" This question is often followed by a very uncomfortable silence. And I wait. The responses I receive are varied. Seldom do leaders answer "yes"; the majority of the time leaders say, "I'm not sure." A few times this question has prompted the leader to call for security and usher me out of the building (just kidding, but I am sure it has crossed the minds of several). When leaders can't answer, we discuss the following questions to help with the answer. Try these questions on yourself:

- Do the people you lead come to you regularly and freely for advice? If not, it is likely they do not trust you.
- Do you get the sense that the people you lead tell you the truth, no matter what the "truth" is without fear of your response? If instead the people you lead don't tell you much or tell you what they think you want to hear, it is because they likely do not trust you.
- Do the people you lead challenge your ideas? Or do they sit quietly and march to your drum; are they a committee of clones? If it is the latter instead of the former it is likely because you are not trusted.

- Do the people you lead openly share their ideas, no matter how absurd they may be? If they are hesitant to explore possibilities, it is likely that they do not trust you and have chosen to operate within the box you have created.

When you as a leader exhibit the following trust Drivers and Attributes you create and sustain an environment where trust will grow over time. Trust promotes trust, and creates an esprit de corps within the organization that brings a shared sense of purpose, drive, and pride among organizational members.

Driver: Extends Trust

ELEMENT	DRIVER	ATTRIBUTES
Trust	Extends Trust	29 > Vulnerability 30 > Sharing Information 31 > Building Confidence 32 > Sharing Power

The chief lesson I have learned in a long life is that the only way to make a man trustworthy is to trust him; and the surest way to make him untrustworthy is to distrust him and show your distrust.

Henry L. Stimson

In the book *The Leadership Triad*, Dale E. Zand discusses the importance of leadership trust in optimizing organizational performance.[1] Zand believes that a leader must extend trust first in order to be trusted in return. As a leader gains trust, cooperation within the organization increases; organizational members are more creative and are more committed. The book also recounts the story of Robert Wood's ability to extend trust. Wood was the head of Sears and Roebuck Co. from 1929 through the mid 1940's. During a train ride, Wood's neighbor Carl L. Odell suggested selling insurance via direct mail, a strategy that had never been done before. Robert trusted Carl, and as a result Allstate Insurance was born in 1931. It was a huge risk but reaped significant results. During the expansion of Allstate, Wood's brought Odell into the company to lead this effort. This is a terrific example of the impact leading with trust can have on leaders, individuals, and organizations.

Leading with trust is really extending trust to those you lead and influence. If you don't first extend trust you will not be perceived as someone who can be trusted; it is that simple. If you are a leader who is always looking over your people's shoulders, calling all the shots (making all the decisions), are highly critical, or are perceived as a leader who believes that your team is incapable and can't be trusted you will not be trusted in kind.

In defense you may say, "But if I don't keep on top of things then people take advantage of me!" And my response is: How often does that really happen? Not often is my guess. And when those situations arise, handle those incidents as they come. Don't make your entire organization suffer. If you lead from a foundation of mistrust, you are likely a person who has trust issues and control issues. Until you recognize that is the case and work through these issues, you will be unable to extend trust. And you will not be trusted.

There are four key attributes associated with Extending Trust. These include:

- **Vulnerability:** Demonstrating vulnerability as a leader.
- **Sharing Information:** Trusting the organization with information.
- **Building Confidence:** Building the confidence of individuals and teams within your organization.
- **Sharing Power:** Sharing power to maximize human capital and capability.

Attribute 29 > Vulnerability

Leaders are not infallible. Leaders don't have all the answers and from time to time make mistakes. After all, leaders are human. If leaders believe that they should have all the answers and can never make mistakes it will be their undoing. Leaders need to show their humanity. One way to show trust is by showing vulnerability.

As a leader, you extend trust by seeking help, by tapping into your organization's talent. Admit that you don't have all the answers. Extend yourself by demonstrating that you depend on those you lead to contribute to finding the answers to the multitude of challenges that come your way. By actually communicating "I need your help," or "I don't know what to do" motivates organizational members to come to your aid. Use the power of communication to extend trust. Trust is not extended through stoic leadership but through actively extending yourself to others.

Leaders also extend trust by showing their vulnerability when admitting to mistakes. This demonstrates integrity. Remember, as a leader you are watched constantly. If you make a mistake, people know it and they talk about it, whether you admit it or not. Frankly, if you don't admit it, they will talk about it even more.

Leaders who take ownership for mistakes and apologize demonstrate trustworthiness. This doesn't require a huge public admission or making a major deal out of how horrible it was and how ashamed you are. It simply requires you to say, "I was wrong and I apologize." Those are powerful words. It is interesting that some leaders find it very difficult to communicate that simple phrase. And yet, that admission and apology is exactly what helps organizational members to perceive a leader with trust. Admitting mistakes moves the organization forward instead of allowing the organization to get stuck talking about the leader's arrogance in not acknowledging the misstep.

Mistakes are the best teacher. In fact, organizations that aspire to create learning organizations actually build learning from mistakes as a core value. How we handle mistakes, what we learn from them, how we grow from the lessons mistakes offer, and how we respond differently to ensure we don't make the same mistake twice is a great value offered for those who are open to learning. Use your own mistakes and admissions as a conduit to show vulnerability, grow your organization, and extend trust.

Attribute 30 > Sharing Information

Individuals desire information from leadership, and it is a leader's responsibility to be a source of information. Leaders who view information as only needed by a few or not needed at all are information hoarders. This is clearly a control behavior. Keeping information from the organization doesn't help achieve organizational goals. Leaders who either do not make the effort to share information or hoard information destroy trust.

Leaders need to provide open channels of communication and access to information that organizational members need to be successful. Organizational members especially need the following kinds of information:

- Information that impacts the organization and therefore organizational members.
- Information that may be helpful to achieving organizational goals, projects, or tasks. Leaders shouldn't filter information and decide what members may find valuable. Let individuals decide what is useful and what is not. Access is what is most important.
- Information on how the function is being perceived by the wider organization. For example, if you as a leader receive a compliment, don't keep it to yourself, broadcast it.

- Information to help organizational members mentally prepare themselves for what might be on the horizon for the organization.

Attribute 31 > Building Confidence

Leaders can extend trust by building the confidence of organizational members.

A few years ago I was communicating with my son a great deal by email. As I inquired about how his studies and work activities were progressing I made a point of always sending him a note expressing how proud I was of him and how much I thought of his achievements. At some point he sent me an email and it said, "I wish you would stop telling me how proud you are of me." Apparently he thought I was sending him too many affirmative messages. I responded by saying I would keep on telling him how proud I am of him as long as I am on the earth and that he is just going to have to get used to it. I also actively look for opportunities to encourage my daughter while she is away at college. I try to keep informed when a big project is due or when she is going to have an exam. I text her or comment on her Facebook page at those times expressing my confidence in how great I know she will do. Each time she acknowledges back with a "Thanks, pops."

Building confidence is accomplished by articulating the belief you have in the abilities of an individual or team. This can be done verbally, in writing, or even accomplished nonverbally (a pat on the back sometimes is all it takes). It doesn't need to be a big extravagant message; it just needs to happen and needs to be consistent and needs to be genuine. Actively voicing confidence is a tremendous motivator and extends trust.

Individuals desire affirmation. Individuals want to know that their leader has confidence in their abilities and that their contributions are appreciated. Leaders who do this are remembered and are trusted. Leaders who don't are remembered as well, but not for the right reasons.

Attribute 32 > Sharing Power

Sharing power across the organization is another form of building confidence. In addition, sharing power extends trust by placing the responsibility and authority on various organizational members. This leverages the intellectual capacity of your organization and builds leadership capability.

Leaders who do not distribute power and instead lead through a command and control style diminish any sense of trust or empowerment within their organization. This style communicates that the leader doesn't trust individuals to make decisions or that they are not responsible to make decisions on their own. This is demoralizing to the organization over time and results in a disengaged workforce.

The leader shares power with organizational members by:

- Allowing individuals to set their own course of action (as much as possible) without interruption. Leaders are perceived with a greater sense of trust when they assume a supportive role (a Driver of Respect) rather than controlling what their people are doing and how they do it.
- Giving individuals the authority to make decisions that are needed to move things forward without delay rather than having to seek your approval. This requires leaders to draw clear authority limits that make legitimate business sense. Doing so will increase productivity and increase your trust quotient.
- Providing input as often as possible that impacts their individual roles or that would leverage their skills.
- Engaging organizational members in solving problems that impact the business. Allow individuals to show added value to the organization by solving business challenges that the organization faces.

A word of caution: once you grant power to someone within your organization, don't take it away. Doing so reverses the trust that you have cultivated. Stay involved, if you need to. Encourage and support. Provide A.R.T.ful feedback as needed (an attribute of Respect). Listen actively to what ideas are being generated, what actions are being taken, how problems are being solved, what opportunities are being uncovered. This will allow you to lead more effectively, increase your leadership capacity, and increase your trust quotient.

Driver: Keeps Confidences

ELEMENT	DRIVER	ATTRIBUTES
Trust	Keeps Confidences	33 > Maintain Confidentiality 34 > Courage to be Candid

Two attributes are associated with Keeps Confidences. The first is for leaders to *maintain confidentiality,* and the second is for leaders to have the *courage to be candid* with the people they lead. Both of these behaviors are instrumental in building and maintaining trust with and among team members. These have tremendous impact on the flow of information that you as a leader will have access to and will directly impact the communication climate of your organization.

Attribute 33 > Maintaining Confidentiality

As you build trust with your team members, they will begin to open up and share information with you. There will be times when you will be asked to keep confidential certain information that is shared with you. Confidential information is information that individuals consider private and meant to be kept between you and them. It is not to be shared with your peers, confidants within the organization, or anyone else. Doing so would break confidence.

Sometimes leaders who are approached with information that is deemed confidential are placed in a precarious situation. Certain information can't be kept confidential. These situations typically relate to Human Resources-related issues. Such information might include breaches of policy, regulatory concerns, matters that place the organization in legal jeopardy, or issues related to employee safety (i.e. harassment allegations). In such instances, as a leader, you will need to explain the responsibility you have as a leader to share the information appropriately. It is also necessary to treat those situations delicately and protect the source of the information when possible. At minimum, ensure that you will protect the individual in stepping forward.

When information is not Human Resources-related, confidentiality must be honored to maintain trust. It is not to be shared with anyone else. When an organizational member has the courage to come to you in confidence, they are trusting that you will not share the information, use it against them, or have it reflect negatively upon them. If the result of sharing the information has a negative impact trust will be broken.

As a leader use the following guidelines when an organizational member approaches you with information deemed confidential:

1. Thank the individual for coming to you and for valuing your discretion.
2. Before the individual divulges the information, explain that you may not be able to keep certain information confidential, if it may have legal implications or relate to the health or safety of organizational members.
3. Assure the individual that you will do everything you can to keep confidence, and if that is not possible, you will do all you can to protect the individual, that the information sharing will not have a negative impact on them.
4. Then, invite the person to share the information.
5. Actively listen. Seek to understand.
6. Proceed with caution and discretion.

Attribute 34 > Courage to be Candid

Gossiping occurs when individuals engage in spreading rumors about other organizational members in order to paint them in a bad light or to make themselves look better. Such information has nothing to do with actual business results. Individuals who participate in gossiping lack integrity and can't be trusted. Leaders who do not stop gossiping and, worse yet, participate in gossiping will lack any level of trust within the organization.

Organizational members desire leaders to set clear standards of conduct. This requires a leader to address issues related to engaging in or spreading of gossip. As a leader you need to set the standard that such behavior will not be tolerated. People will be expected to treat one another with respect and stay focused on what is important to the organization rather than on negativity that gossip generates.

"The Gossip Party"
A Story of Broken Trust

After attending your session where you talked about trust and the need for leaders to remove gossip from the workplace, I wanted to relate my experience on how my leader actually is part of the problem.

During a meeting I had with my boss "Peggy," who is a Vice President, she did something that proved to me why I have such little trust in her. Right before we concluded our meeting she said that she wanted to talk to me about something. Now, I am a very direct person. I am extremely upfront with people, don't pull any punches, and am not afraid to tackle issues head on. I know at times this makes people uncomfortable, but I simply don't allow silliness to get in the way of getting things done

So Peggy says, "Someone told me that you told them that our division lacks good leadership. I was just wondering what you meant by that?" I was absolutely floored. First off, it wasn't true. Secondly, if I had any issues with leadership I would deal with it myself.

I sat there for a couple of seconds trying to figure out how to respond. Clearly, the gossip that is prevalent in the organization, which I refuse to participate in, had gotten way out of control. Quickly it dawned on me where Peggy was getting her information.

About a week prior, one of the worst gossipers in the group, one who can't be trusted as far as you can throw her came to my office. I knew it was trouble as soon as she came in. I immediately shut down. She made idle conversation and then asked me out of the blue, "So what do you think about the leadership team? Do you think it is very strong?" This was a loaded question, and I knew whatever I said would spread like wildfire. So I didn't answer. Instead, I answered her with a question.

I replied, "Why would you ask me such a thing?"

This took her aback because true gossipers are not very smart after all, and she said, "I have heard from others in the department that they don't think that our leaders are doing a very good job, so I was wondering what you thought about it; that's all."

Again, I used caution by merely stating that I had heard similar comments but didn't make it a topic of conversation, since I am so busy (hint, hint . . . stop gossiping). I then said, "It is unfortunate that there is that perception." I was very careful not to say how I perceived the leadership team. However, as a true gossiper, she went off her merry little way, taking my words and twisting them in order to make herself look better. What a despicable individual she is—no integrity what so ever.

So back to Peggy. I said, "That is simply not true. Who told you that?" Peggy told me she couldn't divulge her source. I told Peggy that if someone had attributed such a statement to me that I had the right to know who it was. Peggy again said she couldn't tell me who had told her. Again, I said it was untrue, and I suspected who had been gossiping. I said, "I would like you to call the person in who told you this, and let's have it out right here, right now. I deserve to face my accuser, and trust me, I will get to the bottom of this in short order. No one is going to gossip about me without being held accountable. If you won't stop this, then I will."

Peggy froze. I then turned the conversation by asking Peggy what intent the person would have in bringing this to her attention? What did this have to do with what I was doing for the organization? I was confused. Peggy didn't respond to either of these questions. I also assured Peggy that if I had issues with her or with any other leader that I have enough integrity to discuss any issues I may have directly. I also said that there was a very active rumor mill in the organization, and it was causing a great deal of trust issues in the division. I suggested that this was a prime example of team members spending way too much time talking about one another and too little time actually getting work done. I also suggested that by Peggy believing this nonsense she was participating in the gossiping rather than stopping it. I suggested that it would serve the organization much better if Peggy were to help stop the gossipers and troublemakers who were just making things worse instead of better for everyone involved.

Peggy said nothing.

After the meeting I paid a little visit to my little friend. I said I had just had an interesting conversation regarding something that I supposedly had said about leadership. I said it was unfortunate that such misinformation is tolerated, particularly when the information is a complete fabrication. I then said, "If you can find out who is spreading lies around, let me know, because I would love to have a chat with whoever it is. You see, there are two things that I can't stand, and I learned them both from my mother: I can't stand a liar or a cheat. Apparently we have at least one of these in our midst."

With that I walked away. Since then this individual has avoided me like the plague. When she sees me she won't even make eye contact. I do believe she suffers from a guilty conscience.

Gossiping is an easy trap to be pulled into since it is Machiavellian in nature. Leaders can find themselves engaged in gossip with intentions of trying to improve damaged relationships between individuals within the organization or to improve teamwork. Engaging in gossip will never meet those ends.

As a leader you can quickly identify when someone approaches you with information that is gossiping by asking yourself the following questions:

- Does the information further the business or help achieve an organizational goal?
- Does the information have business implications, or is the information personal in nature and meant to damage someone's reputation?
- Is the information intended to be self-serving on the part of the source of information?

The answers to these questions will determine whether the information being shared contains organizational merit or is pure gossip. If it is gossip, make it stop. Tell the source that gossip is not tolerated in the organization. State that you expect the information not to be shared further. Express that you expect this type of behavior to stop. Be strong, be clear, and be direct. Don't be a "Peggy." Do this and you will demonstrate that you are extending trust to all organizational members by establishing a no gossip zone within your organization.

Another behavior that is closely associated with gossiping is what I call *triangulation*. Triangulation occurs when individuals have an issue with another person, but instead of discussing it with that person, they draw a third person into the situation to create a triangulation effect. Typically the third party is not brought in to mediate the situation, but is used by the individual to talk poorly about the other party involved, in short, to be a gossip partner.

As a leader you need to be clear that triangulation will not be tolerated under your leadership. Instead, set the expectation that your organizational members are to handle issues with one another in a direct and straightforward manner. Not passive aggressively (I have seen it so often I've lost count), not aggressively, not by shutting down, but through a clear, direct, and straightforward approach. As a leader you need to model this behavior first. If you don't know how, learn. Organizational members will mirror their leader in this respect. Communicating and resolving issues between individuals include the following expectations:

- Individuals should resolve issues between themselves without drawing anyone else in the organization into the situation. If the issue can't be resolved, they should seek assistance from their leader for mediation.
- Issues should be discussed in a straightforward manner.
- Individuals should focus on resolving the issue and not on personality differences. Stay focused on achieving organizational goals.
- Address issues that arise when they arise. Don't let issues fester or grow into battles.

As a leader you extend trust by how you set and handle the standards related to confidentiality, gossip, and avoiding triangulation. Set clear standards, engage the organization in open communication, and be an advocate of healthy conflict resolution. This will solidify a sound foundation of trust within your organization.

Driver: Honest

ELEMENT	DRIVER	ATTRIBUTES
Trust	Honest	35 > Clear Standards 36 > Speak the Truth

Being honest is core to trust. A.R.T.ful Leaders exhibit honesty through two attributes: *establishing clear standards of behavior* and *speaking the truth*. Leaders who extend trust by embedding these attributes within their organizations will be perceived with a greater level of trust by those they lead and influence.

Attribute 35 > Clear Standards
Standards of behavior are often established at the company level through a "Code of Conduct" and or through some type of "Ethics Policy." Often organizational members have to read and acknowledge that they understand and will abide by these standards. Beyond this, individuals desire their leaders to set standards of behavior at the organizational level. This is highly important to drive consistency throughout the organization. Consistency promotes trust.

Organizational members desire to understand the expectations leaders have of them. What are the boundaries of conduct that you expect? What do you value? These are important questions to answer and clearly articulate in order to set a framework of consistent behavior within your organization. Without clear standards organizational members will create their own standards of behavior. This leads to inconsistency for not only members within your organization but for those who interface with your organization.

Consider setting standards related to the following areas. Clear standards will impact your operations and the work of your organizational members.

- **Teaming standards:** Consider establishing standards relating to how individuals are to work together or "team" within your organization. How collaborative do you expect your team to be? If you don't set standards in relation to "teaming," this may result in silos within your organization or lead to a lack of cooperation and a culture in which helping others simply does not exist. These are counterproductive and likely if these standards and expectations are not set.

- **Standards for working across the organization:** Establish standards relating to how your organization is to behave when working with other parts of the organization (other departments or functions). What is your expectation regarding the level of service or collaboration you expect of your team? Again, if expectations are not established, how organizational members view this will vary.

- **Service standards:** Establish standards regarding behaviors expected when interfacing with customers (inside and outside the organization). Who are your customers? What are your expectations of "service"? Making service a priority and setting standards will help to create a consistent customer experience.

- **Stewardship standards:** Establish "stewardship" standards. These standards relate to individuals within your organization being stewards of organizational resources. Make clear your expectations regarding the utilization of organizational resources, the relationship with the environment, and corporate responsibility.

- **Management standards:** Establish standards of behavior for your management team (managers, team leads, and supervisors). What expectations do you have for those who have oversight responsibility? How should they view their responsibility (I would recommend A.R.T.ful Leadership!)? Set the expectations. Set the tone. Lead by example.

I recently worked with an organization which, after investigating, clearly had no well-defined standards established by the leader. The lack of standards led to a complete breakdown of communication, a lack of teamwork within the organization, silos, and a lack of trust across the leadership team and across the wider organization as well. Leaders must set standards, standards must make sense, and standards must be communicated and maintained.

Standards set expectations. Expectations bring clarity. Clarity is a conduit to a more trustful environment.

Attribute 36 > Speak the Truth

Organizational members trust leaders who are open and honest. Organizational members desire information concerning what is happening that impacts the company and your organization, as well as their work and their jobs. Leaders who demonstrate a high-level of openness and candor in sharing information and demonstrate the ability to dialogue are trusted; those who do not are perceived with a great deal of suspicion.

Remember that extending trust requires you to trust organizational members with information. As a leader it is important that you are able to be straightforward when communicating. Speak the truth and tell it like it is. When speaking the truth, here are the factors that organizational members will use to evaluate whether you are honest:

- **Are you divulging all the facts?** If organizational members sense you are withholding information they will sense it. So if you can't say everything, then admit it.
- **Are you editorializing?** It is best if you don't.
- **Are you being forthright?** Don't cover up or try and water anything down. Again, people will pick that up.
- **Are you delivering the message with conviction?** Your delivery is key. Communication is an art and a skill that you must master. Leaders who lack the skill to communicate or present effectively will be perceived less positively. Communication effectiveness is a key element of nearly every Trust attribute. If you are not a master in communicating, you need to invest. If you need help, get a coach and develop this skill.
- **Are you providing a feedback channel?** Organizational members want the opportunity to dialogue. Leaders need to provide a feedback channel and be open to having a dialogue with organizational members on issues that are important to them. I realize that there are always a few individuals who make this difficult. Don't allow the few to disrupt the opportunity to dialogue with the masses. To do so is to diminish your trust quotient across the organization. Dialoguing is incredibly important and effective.

Driver: Relationship Builder

ELEMENT	DRIVER	ATTRIBUTES
Trust	Relationship Builder	37 > Cultivate Interpersonal Relationships

Attribute 37 > Cultivate Interpersonal Relationships

The goal of A.R.T.ful Leadership is to create true followership and sustained commitment from those you lead and influence. This can only be achieved by building relationships with individuals within your organization. Building relationships requires the courage to open yourself up to others. When you make this investment it will lead to increased trust as relationships begin to form. As relationships strengthen, commitment increases.

Demonstrating this attribute has a direct implication to the Admiration attribute of being perceived as being *authentic* and the Respect attribute of being perceived as being *fair and balanced*. Therefore, your ability to cultivate meaningful interpersonal relationships is a tremendous influence on your ability to be viewed as A.R.T.ful.

Organizational members desire a relationship with their leader. This begins with you as a leader taking the first step in extending yourself. As the leader you hold the power due to your status in the organization. Therefore, it is up to you to initiate relationship formation with your organizational members. If you do not extend yourself to organizational members, organizational members will be hesitant to extend themselves to you.

Organizational members will perceive you as extending yourself when you do the following:

- **Connect with people at an interpersonal level.** This includes knowing personal information about members of your organization. What are their interests? What are they passionate about? What are their goals (professional and personal)? What motivates them? What are their interests outside of work.
- **Demonstrate genuine interest in what they have to offer to the organization.** What do your organizational members desire to contribute to the organization, and what ideas do they have that may make a positive impact.
- **Listen; really listen.** Take the time to have conversations with individuals within your organization. During these times give them your undivided attention. Conversations are powerful opportunities to create relationships.
- **Personalize rewards and recognition.**

Cultivating relationships requires the attribute of cultivating interpersonal relationships. Building relationships is a process that builds over time. The process can be increased when you engage in self-disclosure and create a positive communication climate that encourages relationships to form.

> **Relationship Process:** When you invest in getting to know organizational members at an interpersonal level, working together becomes easier for everyone. As you establish strong relationships you have the ability to influence organizational members without using the authority of your position, which is much more effective and A.R.T.ful.

Relationship Development Phases Within Organizations[2]

Many relationship theories exist that describe the phases that individuals move through as relationships form and become cohesive. Relationship theory comes from a variety of disciplines, including Organizational Communication, Psychology, Marriage and Family, and Organizational Development. The following phases describe a relationship process in the context of the workplace.

- **Introductory Phase:** During this phase individuals do not know one another. Therefore, individuals are highly cautious in what they say and do. Individuals attempt to put their "best foot forward" in an effort to make a good first impression. A great deal of time is spent on self-filtering and trying to figure out one another. The cautiousness for individuals during this phase is heightened when they are interacting with individuals with greater authority than themselves.
- **Familiarization Phase:** During this phase individuals are picking up cues from one another. Communication is difficult as people struggle to learn how to best communicate to be understood (and not misunderstood). This is the time of much trial and error. This requires transactional contact between individuals. Therefore, leaders must provide opportunities for transactions to occur.
- **Assimilation Phase:** Over time, individuals begin to be more comfortable with one another. Lines of communication begin to open. Individuals learn to adapt to one another's communication style as they become more comfortable in their new environment and with one another. As relationships begin to form, individuals are less self-conscious and careful with what they say and do. During this phase individuals truly begin to step forward and contribute. Leaders should be deliberate in creating an environment where their members are assimilated as quickly as possible in order to maximize talent.

- **High Performing Phase:** Bonds have fully developed. Relationships are valued. This results in complete freedom to communicate openly and honestly. Active dialogues occur frequently, and individuals are highly engaged. Individuals are interested in what one another has to say and are willing to work through disagreements when they occur in order to protect relationships that have formed. Leaders play a major role in whether or not this phase is achieved through establishing a positive communication climate and through demonstrating A.R.T.ful Leadership.

Self-disclosure is key to progressing individuals through each phase of the process. Self-disclosure occurs when you share information about yourself that others would not know unless you told them. When self-disclosure is reciprocal, it speeds up relationship development, because it opens up lines of communication and increases interpersonal understanding. However, not everyone is open to self-disclosure, as the following example demonstrates.

"Relationship Challenged"
A Story of Not Being Open to Self-Disclosure

Years ago when I was first beginning my career, the head of the firm would introduce me to clients somewhat like this: "I would like you to meet Jerry. He will be heading up this project. There is something that you should know about him. If there is someone who will engage in inappropriate self-disclosure it is Jerry." Then he would laugh. The clients would laugh and kind of look at me awkwardly as if how I had been just introduced was actually inappropriate self-disclosure. At the time I didn't think much of it; I just passed it off as one of the many idiosyncrasies of the head of the firm. It really didn't bother me at all.

As I established trust with clients, a few of them would bring up how I had been introduced. I would just pass it off once again as it being part of my leader's personality. Through the years as I built a strong track record with many clients and continued with my career by being the leader of several client relation organizations, I kept thinking about my prior boss. I would use this as an example as I coached my staff on relationship development and what I do to establish strong bonds with clients. When I would recall how my boss would introduce me, my staff would laugh and wonder why he would have ever done such a thing. It would initiate very lively discussions.

As I thought about it, it all made sense. My boss engaged in little self-disclosure and built little trust among his staff. He communicated with his staff very little and made no effort to engage with us. There also was very little camaraderie within the organization.

I have always been very open. It is through my openness and direct style that I believe that I have been able to establish strong client relationships. This was not the pattern of behavior of my boss, so he labeled my style as "inappropriate self-disclosure."

In hindsight what is interesting is that the head of the firm always assigned me to clients who demanded a close client relationship with our firm. My boss knew that I had the ability to connect with people, and I am certain that is why I was always selected for these particular assignments.

I wear my "inappropriate self-disclosure" label with honor. I guess that is why it never bothered me all those years ago. It resonated with me.

Self-disclosure is a key to helping team members understand one another's thoughts, feelings, and preferences. What we value, what we are passionate about, and what our interests are all are dependent on our ability to self-disclose. Also, self-disclosure can be useful in helping teams learn how each individual prefers to communicate, approach problem-solving, and view conflict. This information helps others interact with us more successfully. Self-disclosure also provides an opportunity to provide information about our personal and social lives. This information is valuable in increasing interpersonal understating and is a critical component to forming relationships.

Let's face it, if we just talk business, we don't have the opportunity to actually figure out how to work together as people, because "business talk" is only one dimensional. It doesn't get to our thoughts, feelings, and preferences. Each of us has different comfort levels regarding how much we are willing to self-disclose. The more reticent you are to self-disclose, the more difficult it will be for someone to form a relationship with you, inside or outside of the workplace.

"Clear Lines between Work and Private Life"
A Story of Self-Disclosure

I was asked to work with a leadership team to improve communications and help them with their ability to resolve conflicts more effectively. As part of one of the sessions, I structured a self-disclosure activity. It wasn't anything outrageous; just some basic questions and fun facts that I use to get people comfortable, to open up lines of communication. During the activity one of the leaders shared that she was married and had two children. The room was shocked. None of them knew that she had children. The team had worked together for five years. Then I was shocked. It was baffling to me that this individual had not disclosed the fact that she had two children with her peers. In five years, how you could not mention your children, brag about them at least once, complain about them at least twice (just kidding), not mention a family vacation at least three times, not mention a child's illness at least eight times, not complain about having to go to a child's function at least ten times? Five years; that astounded me. The leader explained she hadn't told anyone because she had very clear lines between her work life and her personal life. The room fell silent.

It was clear that this individual was reticent to self-disclose. This impacted the level of communication that existed between team members. It was apparent that there was a lack of openness within the leadership team. I had my work cut out for me. In a trusted environment, individuals are more likely to self-disclose. I therefore needed to begin to determine what Trust drivers and attributes were missing and therefore inhibiting self-disclosure.

It is essential that leaders engage in self-disclosure with their teams. As a leader you need to step forward and take the lead in self-disclosing. If you do not open yourself to your team, your team will not open themselves to you. If you are reticent to self-disclose then seek help to learn how to begin to open yourself to others. Creating and sustaining effective relationships within your team depends on it. And a word of caution: if ever self-disclosure comes with a punishment it will stop. Never punish or criticize someone for disclosing. You may not agree with what someone discloses, or you may find yourself in "TMI" moments (we all have). But don't judge or criticize. Use your communication ability and leadership presence to handle these "moments" with grace.

Communication Climate

As a leader you can increase trust by creating a positive communication climate within your organization. A positive communication climate begins to open up channels of communication across the organization and impacts positive relations.

According to Adler and Elmhorst[3] the communication climate that exists within the organization will impact organizational commitment and will impact employee satisfaction. The communication climate is based on how organizational members feel about the overall tone of the organization, the level of trust that exists within the organization, and the extent to which relationships have been formed between organizational members.

As a leader you have a great deal of influence in establishing a positive communication climate. Questions you can use to gauge the communication climate of your organization include:

• **Have** relationships formed between organizational members?

- **Do** organizational members engage in open and frequent dialogues with one another?
- **Do** organizational members feel appreciated for the contributions they make towards organizational goals?
- **Do** organizational members work together to solve problems?
- **Do** organizational members use positive adjectives to describe the climate of the organization?
- **Do** organizational members have a sense of pride in being part of the organization?

If the answers to the above questions are not affirmative, it is likely your organization lacks a positive communication climate. It is then your responsibility to take actions necessary to create an environment where trust can increase and relationships can flourish.

Driver: Responsible and Accountable

ELEMENT	DRIVER	ATTRIBUTES
Trust	Collaborative	38 > Leverage Talent 39 > Seek Input

Collaboration is the willingness to lend a hand to other organizational members. Collaboration is a bi-product of an environment that invites open communication, active participation, sharing ideas, and leveraging one another's talents to achieve organizational excellence.[4]

Trust is core to a collaborative environment. Trust opens channels of communication. This frees individuals to exchange ideas and seek input from one another. It is through establishing trusting relationships that individuals actively seek out one another's contributions to achieve outstanding results. Trust is the core to collaboration.

Collaboration unfortunately doesn't happen on a large scale without leadership engagement. A leader needs to determine when to trigger collaboration. Leaders should initiate collaboration by seeking input and leveraging talent from across the organization to achieve the best results. Leveraging talent requires leaders to be diligent at opportunity management. This is a result of having a keen ability to gather the right resources together at the right time to solve the right problems or to take advantage of the right opportunities. Having the insight to know when collaboration is a strategic imperative will increase your value to your team and build trust.

Attribute 38 > Leveraging Talent

Collaboration can only be successful when there is a commitment to leveraging talent. Tapping into talent increases organizational capacity. However, barriers often exist within the organization to block individuals from sharing their talents. When barriers exist, individuals begin to disengage. Leaders have to remove barriers, or collaboration efforts will fail.

As a leader you must scan the environment and remove any of the following barriers that block talent from being leveraged:

- **People blockers:** People within the organization will block one another from sharing their talents. These are power-plays. This is typically driven by the insecurities of individuals. Certain individuals will try to hold back others within the organization from having the opportunity to step forward and be noticed. In certain instances they may even try and discount the talent of others in order to advance their own agenda. As a leader watch for organizational members who are not promoters of leveraging talent. Don't allow this to happen. This will squander talent and stifle collaboration.

- **Talent not recognized:** Individuals may not recognize their own potential. Seek opportunities to tap into untapped talent. Provide opportunities for individuals to stretch their capabilities. Doing this increases capability and builds confidence.

- **Individuals not stepping forward:** When individuals don't step forward and take advantage of collaboration opportunities it likely is due to a lack of trust. If this is a trend within your organization, take action. Trust issues tend to be systemic within an organization at all levels of the organization. Collaboration requires trust. If trust is an issue, you will need to build trust for collaboration to be successful.

Attritube 39 > Seeking Input

Too often I have found that leaders limit the circle of people from whom they seek input in making key decisions or solving problems. I believe this is often a mistake, and our research supports this view. Seeking input is the outcome of championing collaboration throughout the organization. This is demonstrated by continually tapping into the intellectual capital of your entire organization.

Collaboration requires input. Collaborative decision-making and problem-solving leads to better results. By seeking input you ensure that you have considered various perspectives before choosing the best course of action. Diversity in thought increases the quality of options and ultimately, outcomes. Limited viewpoints do not leverage the brain trust of the organization and often excludes the best perspectives.

An A.R.T.ful Leader who has built an organization based on trust seeks input from individuals who are closest to the situation. A.R.T.ful Leaders make sure the individuals who are closest to the situation are included in the discussion. These individuals are critical to the process. Collaboration requires inclusiveness. Seek input from the right people and be as inclusive as possible when creating collaboration opportunities within your organization.

Consistently leveraging talent and seeking input over time begins to create networks throughout your organization. As partnerships are formed and organizational members learn to work together effectively, relationships are formed. As relationships form, trust increases. Through your involvement, your organization begins to function as a high-performing team and you are perceived as an A.R.T.ful Leader.

"What a Difference Trust Can Make"
A Story of Gaining Trust

I report to "Randy," the executive leader in my division. We had a rough start. We just couldn't seem to communicate. He wasn't open. His lack of openness shut me down, I must admit. I was extremely cautious around him. I tend to be a person who others would say "wears his heart on his sleeve." That perhaps has gotten me into trouble in the past. I tend to try and give people the benefit of the doubt. However, with Randy, it was different. I just couldn't seem to connect with him. He was very short with me, and I would even define it as curt at times. I tried to be conversational, but it didn't work. After several months of trying, I started to mirror his communication style.

I didn't trust him. I couldn't. I didn't know who he was, what he cared about . . . nothing. I knew what he expected, and that was a lot. And that was o.k. However, I never knew how I was doing or when I was doing a good job because he was hyper-critical always. He didn't respond to emails or to phone calls and our meetings were short, sweet, and to the point. I need a relationship to really get comfortable, but Randy just simply was not interested.

Once he was irritated at something I had done. I attempted to explain why I had approached the project the way I had, but he was not interested in my explanation. It was his way or the highway. It was something that could have been done either his way or using the approach I had taken. It really was a preference deal, so it was very odd how upset he was.

Once I realized that it was best to do it exactly how Randy wanted things done, I would attempt to preview everything with him and get his approval before moving forward. It was safer that way. This strategy proved to be more successful, but it didn't improve my job satisfaction. My misery index kept creeping up.

The months kept passing very slowly. I had now been working with him for ten months. I had accomplished a great deal, and I had avoided any real confrontation with Randy. Things seemed to be going as well as they could with him. We still hadn't built any type of relationship. Meetings were still brief and to the point. That is why it was such a complete shock when Randy did what he did next.

During a quarterly leadership off-site meeting I was asked to present a component of the agenda. I prepared for the presentation and, as always, offered Randy a chance to review the presentation. I didn't hear back, so I was a bit hesitant. Even so, we had briefly discussed the approach I was going to take, and Randy seemed to be in agreement. At the meeting the presentation went well. Randy sat quietly and didn't seem particularly engaged.

After the presentation Randy stood up to transition to the next topic. But before he introduced the next speaker he said he wanted to say something about me and how we worked together. Randy went on to explain how difficult he found it to work with me when we first started working together. (I wanted to shrink into the carpet). He admitted that he was difficult to work with at times, that he was rigid, and that he was not the easiest to adjust to. He then went on to say how much he had learned from working with me. That through my openness he had learned to be more open. That through my ability to communicate he was beginning to learn to communicate more freely. He also said that he had begun to learn to focus on what was most important rather than what he wanted to happen all the time. Randy said that he had learned how to be more adaptive from working with me. Randy then publically thanked me for my patience with him and for teaching me so much the past several months. He also thanked me for the many contributions I had made to the organization to date and for the contributions that were yet to come.

I was stunned. I had no idea that he had grown as a leader by working with me. Quite frankly, I got the sense that he was just putting up with me. Now looking back at it, I recognize that he was struggling, but struggling to do things differently, not struggling working with me.

After that day I let my guard down. I allowed myself to be more trusting, because Randy had shown that he trusted me. Our relationship took off. We began to work better than ever before. Our relationship became stronger and quite frankly grew into a friendship. We began to share information with one another that in the past we would have never have shared with one another. We entrusted information to one another that we knew would stay between the four walls of Randy's office.

I appreciate Randy greatly. We have become one another's staunch advocates within the organization. We are highly effective at getting things done and enjoy ourselves in the process.

What a difference trust can make.

What I know to be true is this: if you lack the trust of those you lead you will be missing the key to unleashing the true power of your organization. Your people may Admire your achievements and they may Respect your level of accountability and support, but without Trusting you they will be reticent in truly giving their full commitment to the organization. Without trust, you will lack the power of potential.

In my work with leaders I begin by analyzing the leaders' Trust Quotient. Trust is the essence of A.R.T.ful Leadership. Trust is the foundation and impacts true sustained commitment. When leaders struggle with Trust they will struggle with leading a vibrant, healthy, and growing organization. A leader who lacks trust will likely experience churn and burn, whereby the organization members are disengaged, where cohesiveness and collaboration is nonexistent, and talent seeks new opportunities. Focusing on the drivers and attributes of Trust is the springboard for being perceived as an A.R.T.ful Leader.

A.R.T.ful Leadership Reflection Journal

1. What leader have you Trusted and why? What can you learn from their leadership that you can incorporate in your own leadership journey?

2. Which of the Trust Drivers (and Attributes) do you need to strengthen?

3. Who Trusts you as a leader?

4. Who is critical for your success as a leader but may not Trust you? Why? What steps can you take to begin to change that perception?

Creating Synergy through A.R.T.ful Leadership

S ynergy refers to *the whole being greater than the sum of its parts.* This concept has been applied in many disciplines and contexts throughout the ages. When applied to organizations, the concept is really about maximizing resources to achieve results. The degree to which organizations are able to leverage organizational resources effectively will determine how much synergy is created within an organization.

A.R.T.ful LEADERSHIP IN BALANCE

When the concept of synergy is applied to A.R.T.ful Leadership, the focus is on a leader's ability to create a balance within the organization between three distinct organizational elements. By balancing the energy equally, a leader will achieve the proper level of organizational focus, align resources properly, and as a result will create synergy within the organization. The three elements include:

- **Balancing Leader (Self)**: Balance within the organization hinges on the leader's ability to leverage the talents of the Team to achieve Business goals and objectives. This includes the ability to manage the external environment while keeping focus and attention on leading the organization.
- **Balancing the Team**: The emphasis is on the ability of organizational members to operate cohesively, both individually and as a team to meet organizational objectives. This includes leveraging one another's strengths, talents, abilities.
- **Balancing the Business**: This relates to establishing clear business strategies, goals, and objectives. This also includes having a clear direction for what the business does, how the business is defined, and how the business creates an identity to which organizational members can relate.

Organization In balance

An organization in balance is an organization where the Leader, the Team, and the Business are equally balanced to achieve maximum organizational results.

Leader Balance: The leader has defined a clear strategy for the organization and has set clear goals and objectives. The leader has aligned the organizational resources carefully to achieve the business goals. During execution, the leader guides and directs the team to ensure the proper level of support and direction to maximize productivity. At the same time, the leader demonstrates agility by managing the external environment, continuously providing information needed by organizational members to stay focused and productive.

Team Balance: Organizational members have clear roles and responsibilities. Team members work collaboratively as needed to maximize one another's strengths. The team is adept in adapting to challenges and seizing opportunities. Organizational members identify themselves as part of a high-functioning team and feel a sense of pride in team achievements.

Business Balance: Business strategy, goals, and objectives are clearly defined. The expected business results are in harmony with organizational resources. The leader has clearly communicated the Business imperatives to the organizational members, and organizational members understand how their role links to the overall strategy of the business.

Synergy occurs when the Leader, the Team, and the Business are in alignment. Expected results are achieved only when organizational members are highly focused and work collectively. This doesn't happen without A.R.T.ful Leadership creating a true balance within the organization. This balance requires a leader to be Admired, Respected, and Trusted. A leader who is perceived as consistently balancing these three elements will be perceived as A.R.T.ful by those they lead and influence and will also be perceived as a valued leader by the broader environment.

Organization Out of Balance

An organization out of balance does not have the proper alignment between the Leader, the Team, and the Business. These elements are in conflict, which causes stress and inefficiencies within the organization. When out of balance becomes chronic, the organization will lack the ability to create synergy. Without the proper response, leaders will be perceived by those they lead and influence as A.R.T.less.

The Leader is responsible for creating balance within the organization. It is also the Leader's responsibility to take the proper action to return the organization to balance when the organization is not in balance. Ineffective leadership is the main cause an organization is chronically out of balance.

One way leaders cause out-of-balance states is by micromanaging their teams. Leaders who are overly concerned with controlling the Team are unable to monitor the external environment effectively or focus attention on the business. In addition, micromanaging severely inhibits team members from reaching their full potential and reduces productivity.

Leaders also create imbalance within the organization when they have not created a cohesive environment within the team. A lack of coordinated efforts across the team leads to wasted resources. Waste leads to poor quality and rework. This leads to inefficiencies and poor business performance.

Finally, leaders lacking a clear business strategy and direction cause imbalance within the organization. Business goals focus the efforts of organizational members. Without this clarity it is highly unlikely that the organization will be able to utilize resources appropriately. Without a strategy, Leaders will be consumed by trying to create a sense of direction where none exists. Leading an organization via ad hoc initiatives leads to shifting priorities, team conflicts, wasted resources, and ultimately, poor performance.

At times, organizations become out of balance because of changes that force organizational change. When factors cause an imbalance in the organization it requires A.R.T.ful Leaders to determine the proper actions to regain balance and synergy within the organization. The key is for leaders to be cognizant of when change is disrupting the balance within the organization and determine what actions need to be taken to regain balance before the imbalance becomes chronic and hampers the effectiveness of the organization in the long-term. A.R.T.fully managing change is the key to regaining balance and synergy within the organization.

Some of the reasons why an organization may become out of balance due to internal or external environment pressures include the following:

- **Leaders are Self-Absorbed**: Leaders may be focused on self more than on the Team or the Business during times when there are pressing personal matters, during times of intensive professional development, or when the external environment requires their full attention. Whatever the reason, the key during these times is for leaders to keep lines of communication open with organizational members. If leaders articulate the reason why they are focusing on themselves for a time rather than on the Team or Business this will increase organizational understanding. This will allow organizational members to stay focused on business priorities during the time leaders are less attentive.

- **Team Focused on Team Dynamics**: The team may be focused on team dynamics from time to time and be distracted from attending to business priorities. This may be due to organizational restructuring, new management, new roles and responsibilities being introduced to the team, an induction of new team members, or interpersonal conflicts between individual team members or between teams within an organization. Any or all of these pressures cause a disruption in the balance within the team. During these times of instability team members will look to their leader to regain stability and return the organization back to a balanced state.

- **Business Rhythms**: Business rhythms cause an out of balance state. Whether it be budgeting time, strategic planning, or the dreaded performance management cycle (sorry, just being honest), there are times when all your time and attention is on the task at hand, door closed and head down. Other pressing business issues also will require a leader's complete attention, including such things as mergers or acquisitions, organizational expansion or contraction, competitive or customer pressures that require business realignment, and government or regulatory changes, to name a few.

A.R.T.ful Leaders are able to navigate the myriad of business issues successfully by being agile at leveraging the Drivers and Attributes needed to return and/or maintain a balanced state within their organization.

Out of Balance Scenarios

When organizations are out of balance this impacts how leaders are perceived by organizational members. Leaders who are not able to balance themselves as the Leader, the Business, and the Team are perceived to lack A.R.T.ful Leadership capability. *The A.R.T.ful LeaderView 360*[1] seeks feedback from key stakeholders to measure how leaders are perceived in achieving organizational balance. This insight helps leaders determine whether they are perceived as providing the proper level of leadership needed to balance the organization and achieve organizational synergy.

There are various scenarios that describe out-of-balance states. Each state provides a lens to the organization. The longer an organization is out of balance the harder it is for leaders to regain synergy. Chronically out of balance organizations become toxic, and leaders eventually lose the credibility needed to take actions required to reestablish organizational equilibrium.

The following examples represent out-of-balance organizations. Each represents opportunities for leaders to take corrective action to regain organizational synergy. The scenarios presented are derived from working with leaders and leadership teams through various change issues, leadership coaching, and team effectiveness interventions. Each will show how being out of balance lessens the ability of organizations to be productive and the ability for leaders to be perceived as A.R.T.ful Leaders. Strategies are offered to demonstrate how leaders may respond effectively to each scenario.

COWBOY MENTALITY

Cowboy Mentality

Cowboy Mentality refers to a situation in which individual team members' actions and leader actions are not in alignment with the business imperatives. In essence, the human resources within the organization are off doing their own thing and creating their own business priorities. They may be making progress and contributing to the business, but the efforts are disjointed and lack cohesiveness. There is little, if any, collaboration occurring within the team, a situation which leads to competing priorities. The leader is not actively engaged in managing competing priorities. There is a mentality of "I can do it on my own" across the entire organization.

One organization that I worked with took great pride in their Cowboy Mentality. Leadership eventually came to the realization that this was not sustainable. Since the Cowboy Mentality had become a chronic condition across the organization it was not an easy task to break down negative behaviors the Cowboy Mentality created in order to regain synergy.

Cowboy Mentality can be motivated by several forces within an organization. wAll of them may appear to be reasonable, but all lead to inefficiencies and organizational chaos. These forces include:

- **Organizational pressures:** The organization is moving quickly and has aggressive goals. This leads to leaders rewarding ACTION instead of strategically moving the organization towards collective goals. The phase "Fire, ready, aim" becomes the organizational mantra. The aggressive organizational goals preclude team members from working together. Individuals do what they can to complete their assigned tasks as quickly as possible and typically have limited options or resources to change directions if needed. Consequently, organizational members actually work against one another as the environment becomes more and more competitive.

- **Lack of organization resources:** Some organizations lack resources needed by individuals to complete their assigned tasks. Often a subset of the first point, this situation can be the sole motivator of the Cowboy Mentality. Organizations that operate in scarcity motivate individuals to operate independently from one another. Scare resources lead individuals to fend for themselves. This breeds a Cowboy Mentality. When scarcity becomes severe, it begins to bleed into other behaviors. For example, individuals begin to be stingy with their time. People build walls around themselves as a protection mechanism. If anyone looks to leverage someone within the organization they are met with resistance; because organizational members are already stretched, they resist collaborating.
- **Perceived lack of competency:** This harkens back to the A.R.T.less leadership flaw of being The Smartest People in the Room (Chapter 3). The leader and team members simply do not believe one another are competent to get the job done so feel they must do everything on their own. This mentality squanders available talent and completely destroys the opportunity to build capability. Systemically, each individual within the team believes he or she has the best approach and the best solution to everything. In fact, collaborating would just serve to slow things down and annoy.

Impact on A.R.T.ful Leadership

When individuals operate with the Cowboy Mentality they really believe they are focusing on the business. In actuality, organizational members are not leveraging one another's talents. Competing priorities are a constant. This leads to continuous clashes over scarce resources. Unresolved conflicts begin to further divide an already fractured team. The leader is perceived as being ineffective at having the ability to focus the organization, gather needed resources, and leverage talent effectively. Organizational members become frustrated over time by being unreasonably stretched, and they perceive the leader as not being supportive.

When a Cowboy Mentality becomes chronic, the business will underperform. In addition, the leader will not be perceived as A.R.T.ful and will be unable to create and sustain true followership. The leader must begin to focus the organization and realign the resources within the team to be perceived as A.R.T.ful.

STRATEGIES TO BALANCE COWBOY MENTALITY

ELEMENT	STRATEGY	DRIVER	ATTRIBUTES
ADMIRE	Realign the organization to core business goals and objectives.	Deliver Consistent Results	1 > Strategy 2 > Operational Plan 3 > Execute Flawlessly
		Competent	5 > Leadership Ability
RESPECT	Identify team accountabilities to drive business objectives and drive collaboration.	Responsible and Accountable	22 > Sets Expectations 23 > Holds People Accountable
		Provides Feedback and Counsel	25 > Provides Feedback
		Fair and Balanced	27 > Rewards and Recognizes Consistently
TRUST	Open lines of communication (both the leader and across the team).	Extends Trust	30 > Sharing Information 31 > Building Confidence
		Honest	35 > Clear Standards
	Increase collaboration efforts across the organization.	Collaborative	38 > Leverage Talent 39 > Seek Input

"Disjointed"
A Story of Cowboy Mentality

We have a vibrant growing organization. Everyone is passionate about the company, our products, and the possibilities. The main problem that we keep having is that we lack the ability to work effectively as a team, a unit, and as an organization. Each division works independently. Often we go after the same customers and compete against one another. Most of the time we don't even realize it until our customers tell us. Then we have to act as if we know and try to handle very awkward situations. To top it off, we then end up trying to battle one another to see which of our areas will actually have the opportunity to go forward with a particular customer, if we can go forward at all depending on the damage we have already caused. It is a prime example of the left hand not knowing what the right hand is doing.

As we grow, and we are—rapidly—it is getting worse. It is becoming more and more difficult to get anything done. Most of our time is spent trying to figure out how to navigate through all the barriers within our own organization. Who to avoid, which teams to cut out of things, how to work around certain divisions—all counterproductive. It is exhausting. Even within my own team we have no clear alignment. Each of us is off doing our own thing in our own way. It is a recipe for disaster, I'm afraid. Unless we do things differently we are on the road to a complete breakdown.

HIDDEN AGENDA

Hidden Agenda

When a Leader is perceived to have a Hidden Agenda organizational members will view the leader as being self-absorbed and lacking attention to the team or business. A hidden agenda is fundamentally unfair for the rest of the organization because it operates under the surface. Although team members don't know what is going on, they sense that something is going on, and the perception is that whatever it is, it isn't good.

Leaders who are operating with a Hidden Agenda pull back from organizational members. Communication becomes limited, and leaders become evasive about what they are spending their time on. Perhaps a select few may be in on what the leader is up to, but anyone who is privy to what is going on is part of the Hidden Agenda and sworn to secrecy.

A Hidden Agenda has some business implications. For example, if a leader is involved in a reorganization or a merger, the leader will likely be very secretive until the details are able to be communicated to the organization. Although organization members may not know specifics, they sense something is going on and are wary of what it may be and how it will impact them. This is unsettling to organizational members and draws their attention from focusing on the business.

The motivations for Hidden Agendas are many. Some of the motivations of hidden agendas include:

- **Personal Issues**: A leader may be faced with personal issues that require a great deal of attention and energy. These pressures may cause a leader to pull in and withdraw from organizational members until a time the personal issues are resolved. Leaders who are reticent to communicate the reasons (at least at some level) for their lack of focus will be viewed as unfocused and perceived as having a Hidden Agenda.

- **Professional Issues:** There are times when a development focus takes attention away from the Team and the Business. Although this happens rarely, there are certain times or events that require a leader to focus on professional development. If leaders do not clearly communicate that their attention will be on themselves this will disrupt the balance within the organization.
- **Personal or Professional Gain:** Leaders who are focusing on moving up within the organization or leaving the organization often operate with a Hidden Agenda. These efforts require a great deal of time and attention. These are highly confidential in many cases, and the leader is wise to keep this "hidden." The quicker this transition occurs, the better for the team and the business, since the clear focus is not on creating organizational synergy but is on self-promotion or self-preservation.
- **Organizational Politics:** Many times leaders can become embroiled in internal politics that pull attention away from achieving organizational balance. Leaders may give time and attention to politics as they battle for resources or to retain functional control. Leaders embroiled in politics often try to keep this "hidden" and not encumber their organizational members with the organization's "dirty laundry."
- **Leader Competence:** A leader may pull back and withdraw when the Team or Business challenges are greater than their leadership capability. Instead of leveraging the strengths of Team members to meet the challenges, incompetent leaders pull in and sequester themselves, further exacerbating the problems that exist within the organization.

Impact on A.R.T.ful Leadership

Hidden Agendas simply can't achieve the goal of A.R.T.ful Leadership to achieve true and committed followership. Hidden agendas impact the team negatively. The leader has to keep everything secret and private in order to keep their agenda intact, thus building walls between them and their team. As the leader's agenda moves forward, organizational mistrust increases. As trust erodes, admiration and respect soon follows. Leaders who are perceived as having a Hidden Agenda will eventually be perceived as A.R.T.less.

The Communication Driver is critical to being perceived as an A.R.T.ful Leader. Hidden Agendas, on the other hand, deprive team members of communication, further impacting negatively on a leader's ability to be perceived positively.

Strategies to Balance Hidden Agenda

- **Open lines of communication.** Be as open as possible with organizational members, particularly if the reason you are focusing on "self" is due to personal reasons or professional development. This will increase understanding and increase support. This will reduce the amount of energy that organizational members are spending "guessing" what is going on. Remember, organizational members watch you constantly. If you are not communicating, organizational members are making up their own possibilities, and many times these are exaggerated. Communicating with organizational members allows them to get back to focusing on the Business and returns the organization to a more balanced state.

ELEMENT	DRIVER	ATTRIBUTES
Respect	Demonstrate Mutual Respect	19 > Approachable
Trust	Extends Trust	29 > Vulnerability 30 > Sharing Information
	Relationship Builder	37 > Cultivate Interpersonal Relationships
	Collaborative	38 > Leverage Talent

- **Share leadership across the team.** Leverage team members to help share leadership responsibilities. This will allow you to focus your attention on what is important to you at the moment and allow your team to access the leadership necessary to focus on the Business. This will return the organization to a more balanced state and regain greater synergy.

ELEMENT	DRIVER	ATTRIBUTES
Respect	Fair and Balanced	26 > Provides Opportunities to All
Trust	Extends Trust	32 > Sharing Power
	Collaborative	38 > Leverage Talent

- Manage personal and professional agendas as swiftly as possible in order to return attention to leading the Team and the Business.

ELEMENT	DRIVER	ATTRIBUTES
Admire	Represents with Credibility	11 > High Moral Compass 12 > Values 13 > Integrity
Respect	Responsibility and Accountable	21 > Responsible for Own Actions
Trust	Honest	36 > Speak the Truth

"Taking Credit Where Credit Isn't Due"
A Story of Hidden Agenda

Note: This story was shared by an HR consultant. She was asked to increase effectiveness of a team consisting of high-level individuals within an organization. During the process she uncovered a leader with a Hidden Agenda.

I was asked to diagnose the effectiveness of a team and provide recommendations to increase leader effectiveness and collaboration across a large function within an organization. As part of the process I meet with three sets of groups. I identified the groups as "Organizational Advocates"—individuals who were perceived as energetic and completely on-board with the organization; "Disillusioned"—members who had some concerns with what was going on in the organization and because of this their level of engagement and performance had slipped; and "naysayers"—individuals who were extremely vocal about not being happy with the direction of the organization.

I have found over the years that you always find out the most from the "naysayers," and they are often core for any positive change to occur. Individuals were placed in each group by discussing the team members with an internal human resource professional. The individuals who were interviewed did not know which group they had been placed in.

Two of the three "organizational advocates" talked about all the exciting advances that were happening in the business, the challenges that existed, and why it was so important to overcome the challenges to be successful. The third ("David") who was the leader of the team, talked about all the wonderful things he had accomplished, all the wonderful things he had planned to accomplish, and what was going to stand in the way of him being successful. He did this by calling out other organizational members by name and actually disparaging entire departments within the organization (making me wonder at the end of this conversation why he was not perceived as a "naysayer" rather than an "organizational advocate"). I believed I had just come in contact with a Hidden Agenda.

When I met with the "Disillusioned" they expressed their frustration in the lack of collaboration that existed within the organization. When asked what caused the lack of collaboration, they expressed that "certain individuals" had made it difficult to trust one another by pitting team members against each other. They played it safe with regard to naming anyone specifically (trust issue verified). When I pressed them, they mentioned that David tended not to engage his team. This behavior had caused deep divides. My hunch regarding David's Hidden Agenda was starting to be confirmed.

Then I interviewed the "Naysayers." I love hanging with the Naysayers, because if you can get them to talk, you get the skinny on what is really going on. Although they will be negative, many times it is because these individuals are at the end of their rope and simply can't stand it any longer.

In each conversation, David came up. David appeared to be quite a topic of conversation amongst the team. And not only with the Naysayers. I got an earful on how much time was being spent discussing David inside the organization. Matter of fact, one of the individuals called in one of their team members during our meeting to verify some of the information that was being shared.

Each of them described how David seemed to do things to make collaboration difficult between team members. In addition, David's behavior changed dramatically depending on who was present, who was within earshot, and who David was trying to impress. David was a master at managing up and managing across.

David worked very secretively and did not engage the team in anything where there would be potential for visibility. Instead, David would handle it himself, when he shouldn't. He also would set up situations where he would pit team members against one another. David also didn't share information that the team needed, which caused problems in getting things done.

I asked them to provide examples of how David's behavior was received by others in the organization. They described how David had used his political prowess to make the rest of the team look bad and make himself look good. They gave several examples of David doing things to disrupt projects. He would call people out for not getting things done, broadcast that throughout the organization, and then take over and "save the day." This behavior actually had been rewarded by David being promoted, which only resulted in the team being further demoralized.

They had learned to try to stay out of David's way. As a result they lost all confidence in him as a leader and believed that their peers had as well, but were afraid to admit it.

In the final analysis, David's Hidden Agenda destroyed team effectiveness and encouraged similar behavior across the group.

This was a tough message to deliver. I first delivered the findings to the human resource representative and to David's leader in order to gain support for my findings and recommendations—which I received. I am still working on repairing the damage; it is a slow process. I started the process by working with

David to change the way he leads and to work with David's leader to be more engaged with oversight. The issue had become chronic and the damage is deep. The healing continues to be slow, but progress is being made.

It is an interesting psychological phenomenon to justify actions associated with Hidden Agendas, particularly when they are self-serving in nature. At times, individuals may not recognize that they are actually operating under a Hidden Agenda because of a lack of self-awareness. Others simply refuse to acknowledge Hidden Agendas to protect their egos. And between the two extremes there are other motivations. At the end of the day, individuals need to understand the impact that Hidden Agendas have on the people around them and how damaging they can be.

TEAM DYSFUNCTION

Team Dysfunction

In the Team Dysfunction scenario the Team is attending to team issues and are unable to concentrate their efforts on fulfilling Business obligations.

When the team is dysfunctional, the system is out of balance and ineffectual. This imbalance is caused by the following issues:

- **Team or Interpersonal Conflicts:** Conflicts may exist between individuals within the team or between teams within the same function. Interpersonal conflicts left unmanaged can be tremendously harmful to team cohesiveness. Conflicts that are unmitigated often spread as individuals involve other team members. Team members may be pressured to take sides, further splintering the team. As a result, communication within the team collapses and cohesiveness is destroyed. Leaders who ignore this behavior slowly lose leadership control and the ability to focus the energy needed to achieve organizational goals.

- **Leader-instigated Conflicts:** There are instances when the conflicts between teams within an organization or between team members are actually instigated by the leader. Whether done intentionally or not, leaders may pit team members against one another or cause functional teams within the organization to square off against one another by assigning competing priorities (as an example). When the leader is the instigator of the conflict, there is little hope conflicts will be resolved and balance returned.

- **Team Assimilation:** During times when new team members are being formed or introduced into the structure, teams become inwardly focused. The amount of disruption this causes is dependent upon the culture of the organization and the effectiveness of the leader. Organizations that build their cultures on open communication, have established clear norms for collaboration and teaming, and have strong leader support effectively assimilate new team members into the organization. Organizations that lack these elements and lack leadership in actively facilitating the assimilation process will likely experience fractured teams. When teams are not affectively assimilated, team members spend an inordinate amount of time and energy trying to figure out how to work effectively together, and often times, if the culture doesn't advocate working together, may simply not even try. Until team members are able to appreciate one another and learn how to work together they will not leverage one another's talents, which are needed to achieve balance and organizational synergy.

"Taking Responsibility"
A Story of Tackling Team Dysfunction

While working with an organization that included the senior leadership team along with their respective team members, it became very clear that the senior leader of the organization had to make some fundamental changes before team dysfunction would cease and balance return to the organization. It had to start at the top.

I had been asked to work with the organization for several days in a row. At the end of each day I would meet with the senior leader to debrief how things were progressing. In addition, each day began with a session with the senior leadership team. During these sessions it was very evident that this team was extremely fragmented, and this was the cause of the wider issues within the organization.

The senior leadership team had systemic communication problems, lacked cohesiveness, didn't trust one another, refused to engage in open conversation, pointed fingers, and on and on. They also were resistant to change their behavior. The leader sat silent for the most part and when he did speak, he made excuses. What was very clear is that he lacked credibility.

I met with the senior leader and had a frank discussion regarding the organization. Nothing was a surprise; after all, that is why I was there. I turned my attention to what he would have to do for positive change to occur. I introduced him to the A.R.T.ful Leadership Model and to the key Drivers and Attributes that were critical for him to regain credibility and balance inside the organization. He listened and agreed but realized he had much work to do. The first thing we agreed upon was to cancel the remainder of the sessions.

The next two days I worked exclusively with the leader one-on-one. Over the next several months we touched base often as he began to make the changes necessary to assume responsibility and resume leadership of the organization. Once the senior leader had regained credibility, it was time to begin to work with the entire organization to improve effectiveness. It had to start at the top and it did.

Impact on A.R.T.ful Leadership

Leaders who see that their team is dysfunctional and do not take direct responsibility for that dysfunction are delusional. Team dysfunction is a product of a lack of A.R.T.ful Leadership. Making positive and lasting changes to a dysfunctional team takes A.R.T.ful Leadership engagement. Leaders must first look in the mirror and ask: "What is my contribution to my team's dysfunction? What is my obligation going forward to regain organizational synergy?" Only when these questions are asked and addressed will things truly improve.

Leaders who are unable to manage team conflict lose credibility and are perceived as A.R.T.less. Conflicts can generate a great deal of thought diversity when managed constructively and can benefit the organization. Leaders who tell individuals to solve their own problems and step away make a big mistake. Leaders can't turn a blind eye to interpersonal conflicts or team conflicts that remove focus on achieving business results. Instead leaders need to mitigate conflicts and build conflict resolution capability at every level within their organization.

Strategies to Balance Team Dysfunction

During team conflict business attention is ignored and productivity is low; often what work is being accomplished is of poor quality, since individuals lack focus and motivation. When people issues become systemic and chronic, leaders must take responsibility to dramatically change team culture for balance to return. Passivity and passive-aggressive behavior on the part of a leader during team conflicts simply doesn't work.

- **Assertively Manage Team Conflict**: Actively mediate conflicts within the organization. Don't step back and wish it away or tell parties to resolve conflicts on their own, particularly if you notice that the conflict is getting worse or if the conflict has escalated into a "cold war."

ELEMENT	DRIVER	ATTRIBUTES
Respect	Fair and Balanced	28 > Consistently Resolves Issues Fairly
Trust	Keeps Confidences	33 > Maintain Confidentiality 34 > Courage to be Candid
	Honest	36 > Speak the Truth
	Relationship Builder	37 > Cultivate Interpersonal Relationships

- **Communication is Key**: Facilitate open communication and assertive conflict resolution techniques throughout your organization. Conflict is natural and can be incredibility invigorating if managed correctly. Make sure your organization has the skills necessary to take advantage of positive conflict resolution.

ELEMENT	DRIVER	ATTRIBUTES
Admire	Competent	4 > Knowledgeable 5 > Leadership Ability
	Authentic	8 > Confidence
Respect	Supportive	17 > Encouraging
	Demonstrate Mutual Respect	18 > Respectful 20 > Genuine Interest in Others
	Responsible and Accountable	22 > Sets Expectations
	Provides Feedback and Counsel	25 > Provides Feedback
	Fair and Balanced	28 > Resolves Issues Fairly
Trust	Extends Trust	31 > Building Confidence
	Keeps Confidences	34 > Courage to be Candid
	Honest	36 > Speak the Truth

- **Set Expectations for teaming**: Expect organization members to work together, collaborate, and share information. Hold people accountable for these expectations.

ELEMENT	DRIVER	ATTRIBUTES
Respect	Responsible and Accountable	21 > Responsible for Own Actions 22 > Sets Expectations 23 > Holds People Accountable
	Provides Feedback and Counsel	24 > Seeks Feedback 25 > Provides Feedback
Trust	Honest	35 > Establish Clear Standards 36 > Speak the Truth

- **Assimilate Teams and Individuals**: Keep engaged as the leader and make sure organizational members are involved during the time teams come together and individuals are introduced to the organization. Invest in integrating teams and individuals properly. Create an environment where organizational members have the tools, resources, and time needed to feel welcomed and grounded in the organization.

ELEMENT	DRIVER	ATTRIBUTES
Admire	Represents with Credibility	13 > Integrity 14 > Reputation
Respect	Supportive	16 > Dependable 17 > Encouraging
	Demonstrate Mutual Respect	19 > Approachable 20 > Genuine Interest in Others
Trust	Extends Trust	30 > Sharing Information
	Relationship Builder	37 > Cultivate Interpersonal Relationships

"The Bullies"

Story of Team Dysfunction

When I first arrived at the organization I met with the leader privately to discuss the dynamics of the team. "Tom," the leader, told me that his leadership team consisted of three directors and seven managers. Tom had been the senior leader for three years. Two of the directors had been with the company longer than Tom. Four of the mangers had only been with the team three months. The team had experienced 60% turn over the past year. Each member of Tom's team was responsible for different areas of operations, but their areas of responsibilities often crossed.

When asked to describe the current team dynamics, Tom said that the team was not on speaking terms. He attributed this primarily to the two directors that had been with the organization the longest. Tom told me that the two directors "ran the ship." He said that they were very tough on team members. Tom explained that they were very aggressive. They were argumentative, and they shot down any new idea that fellow team members had with an attitude of, "We've tried that and it doesn't work!"

When I asked Tom what he had done to mediate or reign in the two directors, he sat silent. He beat around the bush for a bit, but it was clear that these two also dominated Tom as well. Tom said that all his time was spent calming people down, listening to grievances they had about the two directors. Tom also spent a great deal of time fielding questions team members had that they couldn't get answered by the two directors. Finally, Tom spent time trying to talk team members from leaving the organization.

Tom explained he depended upon the two directors a lot despite all the problems; they were knowledgeable and got a great deal done. I reminded Tom that he was experiencing 60% attrition by doing nothing, and I asked him to consider what the impact was on the organization.

After hearing about what was going on I told Tom that it was time that we get to work. I presented him the A.R.T.ful Leadership Balance model and had him "draw," or diagram, the balance of his team. Not surprisingly, it mirrored Team Dysfunction.

The strategy started with Tom. Working hand-in-hand we devised a set of expectations for how Tom expected the team to function going forward. Once they were clear and Tom was ready to stand behind them, we moved to step two.

The next step was to have meetings with each team member. We crafted a communication that was sent to the team. The communication explained the goal of the work that Tom and the team were embarking on and invited them each to the meeting. During each meeting Tom and I communicated verbally the goals of the work and walked through the process that would be used (including several leadership sessions). We then asked each leader what they thought about the process and if they had any questions or concerns. This approach was used to get a sense of how receptive each member of the team would be working through the process. Interestingly (or not), everyone except the two directors causing the most difficulties were extremely excited about the opportunity.

Tom and I then prepared for the first group session. During the first session, I would have Tom present the overview of how we had gotten there, where we were going, and the process to getting there. I would then have him move to his expectations for "teaming." Finally, Tom would explain his role as the leader and what they could expect from him. All of this was a dramatic departure of what the team had experienced before.

When the complete agenda was set for the first meeting, we scheduled the meeting and sent out the invite to the team members. The next day I got a call from Tom. One of the problem directors had declined the meeting invite and had turned in a resignation. It appeared that the director was not prepared to do things differently. Tom was not surprised and was actually relieved.

The sessions and subsequent work with Tom and the team went well. Tom learned how to use A.R.T.ful Leadership to achieve team balance. Team members responded with energy and passion. The remaining problematic director was not responsive at first and hesitant. However, over time, this individual became part of the new functioning team and was a valuable asset moving forward.

"The Wake Up Call—The Meeting from Hell"
A Story of Team Dysfunction

I brought my team together to reinvent how we conducted operations. This would require my three corporate managers and three field managers to begin this work.

During the first day of the three-day meeting, I presented the goals of the meeting and the agenda. I provided a high-level overview of where we needed to go. I explained that I wanted this to be owned by them since they would have to manage the new processes. Therefore, I wanted them to work together to devise what "new" looked like, so they were comfortable going forward.

I then provided some parameters and answered questions. I told them that in the morning we would reconvene, I would review their ideas, and then we would move on from there. I told them that if they needed anything I was available via my cell phone. They seemed to be excited to get started. With that, I left them to work.

The next morning as they entered the room I could tell by their body language that they were not as excited as the day before. They weren't speaking to one another—at all. Only one of them said "hello" to me, although I greeted each one of them. As each of them took their seats, they quickly took out their laptops and began working. The room was eerily quiet.

When everyone finally arrived (Greta and Sara where fifteen minutes late), I called the meeting to order. The usual attentive and lively group made no eye contact with me or one another. Greta and Sara were not paying attention to me; they just kept working on their computers, doing email I assumed. I ignored this for the time being in hopes that they would come to their senses and join the meeting.

I reviewed the agenda for the day and made some general opening remarks stating how excited I was for the opportunity to work as a team to define our organization's future . . . nothing. Since Sara and Greta were still not paying attention, I very politely said that computers wouldn't be needed and everyone could put them away. With this, everyone except Greta put away their computers. Greta kept working on her computer.

The tension kept rising as my team kept looking at Greta and then back to me to see what I was going to do. I was wondering the same thing. You could hear a pin drop. Greta was slouched down in her seat and still had her coat on. . . . Nonverbal messages, anyone? Again, I ignored Greta, hoping she would soon begin to act like an adult. I would soon find out I was very wrong.

I asked the group to take me through what they had come up with the day before. No one said a word. I once again said, "Who would be willing to give me a progress report from your work yesterday?" Again, silence.

Sarah finally spoke up and said she would recap. She began to describe some of the things the team worked on and how difficult it was for the team to agree on anything. Her description was very polite, and she was hesitant, but at least she was letting me know what had happened. I could tell that Sarah was afraid how the team would react.

Since Sarah was the only one talking, I started to ask her questions to gain more perspective. This is where things started to really get nasty. Everything that Sarah said, Carla started to jump in and correct. I started to get the sense that Carla may have been part of the problem.

With each passing moment the room was growing more tense. I knew there were some tensions between Carla and some of the other team members, but never anything like this. In particular, I knew that Carla and Sarah often had trouble working together, but had never found them to be hostile towards one another, particularly when the entire team was together.

The unraveling of my management team was really shocking to me. I had one team member with her face buried in her laptop, two team members verbally sparing over what had occurred the previous day, and the other team members had completely checked out. I was paralyzed.

All of a sudden Tami started to cry and ran out of the room. No one had said anything to her; neither Carla nor Sara had mentioned her name. She had not said a word at this point since entering the room. She just started to cry and ran out.

Tami's tears seemed to inflame both Sara and Carla. They literally started to scream at one another. After about ten seconds I finally couldn't take any-more and yelled, "ENOUGH!" The room froze. I was even surprised. Then Sarah started to cry and she ran out. Then, Carla got up and stormed out of the room. Three down, three to go.

I tried to regroup. I know . . . about time, right? I once again tried to find out what had happened the day before. I had to get to the bottom of it. I had a feeling that the key problem areas may have left the room, except for Greta, perhaps. I finally told Greta to put her computer away; I was done.

I had the feeling that the two remaining field managers were not going to be open while Greta was present, but I tried anyway. I kept asking questions and sat in silence until my questions were answered. It didn't take long before Greta stood up and left the room. It was exactly forty minutes into Day Two of our meeting.

I will cut it short and give you a synopsis of what happened from this point. For the next hour only the two field managers were in the room. They told me what had happened the day before. It was complete chaos. Greta, one of my corporate managers, and Carla, a field manager basically kept fighting for control. Because of this nothing was accomplished. They also told me that the team had been splintered for months, yes months. Being in the field, these two managers were able to keep away from the team issues for the most part but dreaded any time they had to try to work as a management team. They explained that Carla was a control freak, and if it wasn't her way, then she didn't like it and simply would not want to cooperate. Since they had to work with Carla closely they found themselves having to pick sides often. It was very difficult for them.

By noon, everyone but Carla had returned to the room. Carla didn't return the entire day. I didn't hear from her, and she didn't return my phone calls or emails. I sent her an email at the end of the day saying that she was to be in my office at 8:30 the next morning and not to be late.

That night I realized that I had to make some serious changes to get the team back on track. As the leader I had ignored deep problems that existed in the team for a very long time. It was my responsibility to set the tone and make sure my team was successful. I had heard the complaints from my team over the past months but had told them each to work it out. Clearly they couldn't, and I should have recognized that. I had to take ownership for not being more involved and stopping the behaviors that I knew were disrupting the team.

I made a list of behaviors that would no longer be tolerated by anyone on my team. I created a list of expectations I had for my team for working together and for behaviors expected during leadership meetings.

The next day I called each manager into my office individually to review the behaviors. I began each of the meetings by apologizing for my part in the dysfunction of the team. I promised each team member to be engaged and to provide leadership going forward. I challenged them to call me out if they saw me not fulfilling my leadership obligation. I made it clear what would and would not be tolerated. I made it clear that from this day forward I had a "zero tolerance" policy for bad behavior. Consequences were clear and severe. What happened the previous two days would never happen again—never.

The conversation with Greta, Sarah, and Carla was interesting. From that day forward they did not behave badly when working together or in team meetings. If similar behavior had happened, there would have been consequences, and everyone knew it. The managers may not have been best friends, but they were able to work together effectively and keep focused on achieving business objectives.

Business Paralysis

BUSINESS PARALYSIS

In the Business Paralysis scenario the majority of the focus is on the Business itself due to the number of business priorities that that have been established. Leaders are being pressured to respond to a multitude of business demands. This constant pressure causes stress on Team performance and leads to inefficiencies in productivity and the ability for Leaders to achieve balance.

When Business priorities are draining organizational resources, the Leader is perceived as ineffective and unable to create a strategy that is realistic and achievable. Over time organizational members become stressed and exhausted with the constant Business pressures they face, and attrition is likely to increase.

When Business is out of balance with the Leader and the Team it may be due to the following:

- **Unrealistic Business Goals**: The organization has set strategies that are too aggressive and / or has established too many business goals in relation to available resources. The constant pressure of attempting to reach the goals actually becomes a detractor rather than a focus and motivator to the Leader and Team. In a constant effort to perform at higher and higher levels, performance and quality begins to slip.

- **Changing Priorities**: If everything is important, nothing is important. When the Business is under pressure, there tends to be a constant shift in priorities within an organization. If Leaders are not deliberate in creating a clear roadmap for the organization this may occur. Leaders who are reactive will keep adding priorities to the Team. Leaders without a clear focus stretch organizational resources to the breaking point in an attempt to accommodate multiple demands.
- **Volatile Environment**: Changes in the external environment due to customer demands, political or regulatory changes, wider organizational changes, and/or competitive pressures may require a Leader to focus their attention and resources on the Business. During these times, Leaders must leverage and deploy their organizational resources carefully to be effective and efficient.

Impact on A.R.T.ful Leadership

Leaders who place Team members in an environment where they are constantly faced with trying to satisfy unrealistic Business expectations are perceived unfavorably by the Team. This perception is exacerbated when Leaders are unable to provide resources needed by the Team to meet the Business demands (people resources, information resources, technology resources, time). Extreme business demands coupled with an environment of "scarcity" is a perfect storm for a Leader to be perceived as A.R.T.less.

When a leader is able to leverage resources appropriately and stay engaged with the Team during times when the Business requires attention, the Leader will be perceived more positively. Leaders who have the ability to lead the organization through times of adversity by providing the proper level of guidance and direction are more likely to be perceived as A.R.T.ful.

Strategies to Balance Business Paralysis

- **Establish a Strategy and Prioritize**: First, have a strategy that is achievable. Next, set clear and specific priorities for the organization. Have a plan and stick to it. If necessary, tweak it but don't throw it out or ignore it. Flexibility is important, but so is having a plan.

ELEMENT	DRIVER	ATTRIBUTES
Admire	Deliver Consistent Results	1 > Strategy 2 > Operational Plan 3 > Execute Flawlessly
	Competent	4 > Knowledgeable 5 > Leadership Ability 6 > Tenacious Drive to Succeed
	Social Dexterity	7 > Networking
	Authentic	8 > Confidence 9 > Connections
Respect	Supportive	15 > Loyal 16 > Dependable 17 > Encouraging
	Responsible and Accountable	21 > Responsible for Own Actions 22 > Sets Expectations
	Fair and Balanced	27 > Rewards and Recognizes Consistently
Trust	Extends Trust	32 > Sharing Power
	Collaborative	38 > Leverage Talent 39 > Seeks Input

- **Resource Appropriately**: Ensure that the organization has the resources needed to achieve the established business goals.

ELEMENT	DRIVER	ATTRIBUTES
Admire	Deliver Consistent Results	2 > Operational Plan 3 > Execute Flawlessly
Respect	Supportive	16 > Dependable
Trust	Collaborative	38 > Leverage Talent 39 > Seeks Input

"Who's on First"?

A Story of Lack of Priorities

My team and I are exhausted. Our leader is out of touch with reality. There doesn't seem to be a plan in place for anything we do. As a result it is utter chaos in our department. Our leader "Kyle" has set aggressive goals for our management team. I understand that. Our organization is faced with increasing pressures from our competition. I get that too. The problem is that Kyle keeps changing his mind. It has gotten so bad that the management team doesn't know what to do next because of the switching priorities.

The last month has become unbearable. Kyle has decided to have daily "huddles" to review the business. During these meetings he makes directives on what each of our teams should be focusing on for the day. Yes, the DAY.

During the morning meetings we are to provide him with an update on the various projects that our teams are working on. Kyle never listens; he interrupts and goes off into tangents and starts talking about why we should not be doing certain things any longer, because he heard about something else more important. We try to explain that to shift attention away from what our teams are doing will delay important work that needs to be done. But Kyle won't have it.

Kyle then tells us what we should be doing for that particular day. If we are lucky, some of us are able to stay the course for a week at a time. Often we have to go back and stop our teams from doing what they are doing and realign them to other work. The constant disruption is causing major problems with the team. Many of the management staff is experiencing increased absenteeism, and productivity is really getting bad.

Kyle eventually comes back and tells us to get back to what we were doing prior to stopping us. These constant stops and starts have led to increased inefficiencies within the organization. It seems that we can't get anything done. The stress is increasing as confusion between the management and our team members increases. Kyle needs to get it right real soon. In actuality, none of us believe that Kyle has the ability to do so.

A.R.T.ful LEADERSHIP IN BALANCE

Achieving Balance

Creating synergy within the organization by balancing the Leader, the Team, and the Business is essential for being perceived as an A.R.T.ful Leader. Harmonizing these forces within the organization capitalizes the organization's potential. As a leader it is important that you continuously analyze the balance within your organization.

Your leadership intuition should be a guide to when your organization is out of balance. If you sense that things are out of balance, take a moment and honestly assess the balance within your organization. In addition, seek input from others whom you A.R.T. in order to get where you need to be. The key is to seek a balance between how you Lead the organization, the Team, and the Business.

When you believe that things are out of balance, it is important to take the following steps:

- **Analyze the balance.**
- **Identify reasons why it is out of balance.**
- **Determine the necessary actions to attain balance to achieve synergy.**

By consistently following these steps you will be perceived as a leader who has the ability to create and sustain a high-performing organization. This requires you to continuously leverage a diverse set of A.R.T.ful Leadership drivers to be successful.

A.R.T.ful Leadership Reflection Journal

1. Describe a time when you have been in an organization that has been out of balance. What did the leader or leaders of the organization lack that created imbalance? What can you learn from that experience to ensure that you do not create the same imbalance within your organization?

2. What is the current balance within your organization? Assess your ability to equally balance your role as a Leader, lead the Team, and lead the Business. Is your organization in balance? Below, circle the the diagram that you perceive exists between Leader, Team, and Business in your situation. Be honest. If out of balance, identify the reasons that are causing the imbalance and actions needed to achieve synergy.

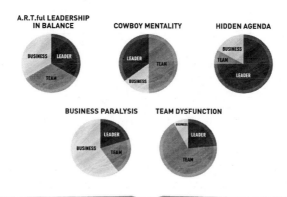

Power and the
Impact on A.R.T.

Power is neither inherently good nor bad.
It is how it is used or abused that makes it so.

Anonymous

When looking at how to improve leadership ability, the question of how to influence and motivate people effectively always becomes part of the discussion. This was the key question used in analyzing data and identifying the key A.R.T.ful Leadership Drivers and Attributes that contribute to a leader creating true and committed followership.

As a leader you are continually influencing others both inside and outside the organization. How you choose to influence will have a direct impact on how you are perceived as a leader. The more you are able to flex how you utilize your power and influence, the more effective you will be at being perceived as A.R.T.ful.

As a framework to explore the notion of power and influence, I am borrowing from a well-known study on power and influence. Since it was published, the framework has been widely accepted as a management theory and appears in many management and leadership textbooks. It is being used here to set context and to discuss power and influence in relation to A.R.T.ful Leadership.

In 1956 social psychologists John French and Bertram Raven[1] explored how individuals use power and communication to influence the behavior of others. As a result they identified the five bases of power that are used to influence.

Legitimate Power—Influencing others through your status or position.

Reward Power—Influencing others by providing them with rewards.

Expert Power—Influencing others by what you know or by your expertise.

Referent Power—The power to influence through one's social abilities, charm, or charisma.

Coercive Power—Forcing someone to do something against their better judgment by some type of intimidation or threat.

What follows is a discussion on each of the five bases of power, how each impacts A.R.T.ful Leadership, and which A.R.T.ful Leadership Drivers and Attributes align with each power base (if there is alignment). Doing this analysis will enable you as a leader to be more diligent in flexing power and influence within your organization and doing so A.R.T.fully.

Legitimate Power

Legitimate Power is also referred to as "positional power," This is a leader using the power of their position to influence and using authority to motivate. It is the power of the organizational chart. It is the authority that a boss has over their direct reports. Legitimate power includes certain types of authority that leaders have: hiring, managing performance, conducting reviews, giving direction, setting organizational strategy, managing resources, and managing operating budgets. Organizations also establish Legitimate Power through establishing authority limits within the organization. These include spending limits and which roles can enter into contract obligations, for example.

Legitimate Power: Impact on A.R.T.

Leaders use Legitimate Power constantly by the very nature of their positions. And because of their position, leaders are constantly being watched and scrutinized by those they lead and influence. Therefore, the impact of Legitimate Power on A.R.T. is unavoidable. When leaders misuse or abuse of their authority or position it can cause negative impressions of their leadership ability.

Organizational members may respect someone's Legitimate Power, but this doesn't mean they necessarily respect them as a leader. The level of A.R.T. the leader receives is dependent on how they execute their Legitimate Power. Legitimate Power brings with it responsibility to devise a strategy and execute on that strategy; responsibility to plan and budget for necessary resources;

and responsibility to lead, leverage, and develop the human resources needed to meet organizational expectations. Doing all of these will determine whether a leader has the ability to use their Legitimate Power appropriately. Doing all these exceptionally well will determine whether a leader will be perceived as A.R.T.ful.

Legitimate Power Aligned with A.R.T.ful Leadership

It could be argued that all the A.R.T.ful Leadership Drivers and Attributes link to Legitimate Power. However, when isolating only the legitimate authority of a leader due to the position within an organization, the A.R.T.ful Leadership Drivers and Attributes become more defined. The following are the direct Drivers and Attributes that are associated with Legitimate Power. (For more on the A.R.T. Drivers and Attributes, see chapters 4–6.)

LEGITIMATE POWER DRIVERS AND ATTRIBUTES

ELEMENT	DRIVER	ATTRIBUTES
Admire	Deliver Consistent Results	1 > Strategy 2 > Operational Plan
	Competent	4 > Knowledgeable 5 > Leadership Ability
Respect	Supportive	16 > Dependable 17 > Encouraging
	Responsible and Accountable	21 > Responsible for Own Action 22 > Sets Expectations 23 > Holds People Accountable
	Provides Feedback and Counsel	25 > Provides Feedback
Trust	Extends Trust	30 > Sharing Information
	Honest	35 > Establish Clear Standards
	Collaborative	38 > Leverage Talent

A.R.T.ful Leadership Reflection Journal

1. When have you used Legitimate Power incorrectly, and what was the impact to being perceived as an A.R.T.ful Leader?

2. How could you have done things differently?

Reward Power

Leaders use Reward Power to influence by providing something to organizational members that they desire. Organizational rewards can take many forms, including promotions, raises, stocks, or even gift certificates, to name a few. Recognition is also a form of reward that leaders often overlook.

When using Reward Power, leaders should consider the following:

- **Monetary** rewards, although important, are fleeting in nature as an influencer or motivator for an extended period of time.
- **Recognition** is highly motivational and is appreciated by individuals when used consistently and genuinely delivered.
- **When** possible, rewards have the most impact when they are personalized. This shows that you understand what is of greatest value to the individual (and therefore influence and motivate the individual). For example, if you give a monetary reward to an individual it may not provide a positive influence. If instead you provided the same individual with more time off work, this may be perceived as having greater value and will have a tremendous influence on the individual.

Reward Power and the Impact on A.R.T.

Consistently rewarding and recognizing members is a highly effective motivator and influencer. This should include recognizing individuals and teams for making contributions towards goal achievement. In addition, leaders should look for opportunities to recognize individuals for making positive contributions to the organization in other ways, such as contributing to team cohesiveness and making positive contributions to the culture of the organization.

When leaders go out of their way to acknowledge and reward contributions outside of the normal organizational cycle (during performance management), it is highly motivational. Leaders need to be mindful of focusing their attention on being creative in structuring a reward system that operates within the organization's budget and that will have a positive response from organizational members. Rewards do not have to be of high monetary value to work, but they do have to be meaningful and valued by individuals. If it doesn't carry value, it will miss the mark.

Leaders should be cognizant about rewarding individuals through continuous appreciative feedback. Simply thanking people for their efforts, telling people that they are doing a "great job," and other simple gestures of appreciation go a very long way. Recognizing individual's contributions builds confidence in team members. As confidence increases so does the desire to perform. This in turn builds a greater sense of engagement and commitment to the organization and to you as a leader.

On the other hand, Reward Power has a negative impact on A.R.T.ful Leadership when organizational members perceive that rewards have been taken away from them or when leaders do not acknowledge contributions. Both of these scenarios can be highly disruptive or discouraging to organizational members. They destroy the motivation of organizational members and impact a leader's ability to affectively influence.

> **Taking Away Rewards**: Organizational members are very sensitive to changes made to the compensation structure, whether it involves pay, benefit restructuring, or other changes in compensation that reduce total employee compensation. Such changes are highly scrutinized by employees and are a main topic of conversation inside the organization and at home. These changes impact the financial health of organizational members. Although a leader may have no direct authority in changes that are made, it will reflect negatively on the leader. Why? Because the leader is the face of the company for organizational members and at some level will be the conduit to communicate changes to organizational members. When these changes are not also replaced with other incentives that may be of benefit to employees, organizational members will likely become lees engaged and committed to the organization and to the leader.

> **Not Recognizing Contributions**: Leaders who fail to recognize their people properly by ignoring contributions or by taking credit for the team successes themselves will not be viewed as A.R.T.ful Leaders. In fact, this Flaw of A.R.T.less leaders is discussed in Chapter 2 (Flaw #7). A leader who views significant contributions as simply being a requirement of having a job will likely not engage in appreciative feedback. Such leaders will lack the ability to influence organizational members positively (refer to "Unaware" story in Chapter 5 for an example of the impact this has on organizational members).

Reward Power Aligned with A.R.T.ful Leadership

A.R.T.ful Leaders are appreciative and recognize that success is only achieved with and through others. A key element in achieving A.R.T.ful Leadership is to reward and recognize organizational members consistently and fairly. Leaders who understand this and work to achieve this end will be viewed favorably.

Leaders appropriately leverage Reward Power by demonstrating the following A.R.T.ful Leadership Drivers and Attributes:

REWARD POWER DRIVERS AND ATTRIBUTES

ELEMENT	DRIVER	ATTRIBUTES
Respect	Supportive	17 > Encouraging
	Demonstrate Mutual Respect	20 > Genuine Interest in Others
	Feedback and Counsel	25 > Provides Feedback
	Fair and Balanced	27 > Rewards and Recognizes Consistently
Trust	Extends Trust	31 > Building Confidence

A.R.T.ful Leadership Reflection Journal

1. When have you applied Reward Power correctly to influence positively?

2. When have you used Reward Power incorrectly, and what was the impact to being perceived as an A.R.T.ful Leader? How could you have done things differently?

Expert Power

Expert Power is based on leaders influencing others through expertise. Sharing expertise can take many forms, including sharing knowledge of the company, sharing technical ability, and/or sharing a wide-array of other expertise that you possess as a leader.

Expert Power and the Impact on A.R.T.

When leaders apply Expert Power correctly it can positively impact how the leader is perceived. A.R.T.ful Leaders utilize Expert Power to improve the ability of organizational members to perform and aid in the development efforts of their team. These are primary ways in which Expert Power positively influences organizational members and contributes to a leader being perceived as A.R.T.ful.

Sharing Expertise to Aid in Goal Achievement: When leaders share expertise needed to achieve organizational goals or complete tasks it is deeply appreciated by organizational members. Leaders who stay engaged and provide guidance and direction by offering expertise demonstrate that they are committed not only to organizational success but individual success as well.

Sharing Information: Leaders have access to information that isn't available to their team. Therefore, organizational members rely heavily on leaders to be the conduit of information they need to be successful. When leaders actively share information and knowledge with their organization, it increases their value and credibility. This opens lines of communication, which is critical to a vibrant organization. Communicating and sharing information are key factors in increasing expertise and knowledge in the team and increasing your influence as a leader.

Developing Others: Leaders have a tremendous opportunity to influence by participating in the development of individuals within their organization. Sharing expertise through coaching and mentoring is a powerful influencer and motivator. When leaders invest their time to develop organizational talent they not only build commitment and loyalty, but they also are increasing organizational capacity.

Leaders may abuse Expert Power by over-directing or controlling the organization. When a leader believes that they are the sole Expert within the organization they begin to block others within the organization from fully participating in the functioning of the organization. When leaders don't leverage organizational strengths and talents, it leads to disengagement.

Leaders also need to avoid the trap of believing they are too busy to share their expertise or participate in the development of their people. This is an excuse that leaders often make in participating in the development efforts of their people. By squandering these opportunities leaders lose the opportunity to build leadership capability within their organization. The fact is, when development is done correctly, time should not be a factor that stands in the way of leaders sharing their expertise

Expert Power Aligned with A.R.T.ful Leadership

Leaders exert Expert Power by demonstrating the following A.R.T.ful Attributes and as a result will positively influence organizational members and build organizational capacity:

EXPERT POWER DRIVERS AND ATTRIBUTES

ELEMENT	DRIVER	ATTRIBUTES
Admire	Competent	4 > Knowledgeable 6 > Tenacious Drive to Succeed
Respect	Supportive	15 > Loyal 16 > Dependable 17 > Encouraging
	Demonstrate Mutual Respect	19 > Approachable 20 > Genuine Interest in Others
Trust	Extends Trust	30 > Sharing Information 31 > Building Confidence 32 > Sharing Power
	Collaborative	38 > Leverage Talent

A.R.T.ful Leadership Reflection Journal

1. When have you applied Expert Power correctly to influence positively?

2. When have you used Expert Power incorrectly, and what was the impact to being perceived as an A.R.T.ful Leader? How could you have done things differently?

Referent Power

Referent Power is influencing through an individual's social ability, personality and charisma. A leader who possesses Referent Power attracts others through their ability to connect with people and to create interpersonal relationships. Leaders who exercise positive Referent Power are often seen as role models, and individuals seek to emulate them and adopt similar qualities. Leaders who influence with Referent Power are skilled communicators, are socially adept in a variety of situations, and are highly engaging.

Referent Power and the Impact on A.R.T.

Leaders who possess the ability to influence via Referent Power have a positive impact on their ability to be perceived as A.R.T.ful Leaders. The characteristics and qualities of Referent Power touch each of the elements of A.R.T.ful Leadership.

A.R.T.ful Leaders who are Admired demonstrate Referent Power in their ability to network with others successfully and in having confidence to make authentic connections with individuals both inside and outside the organization.

A.R.T. Leaders who are Respected demonstrate genuine respect for others and are genuinely interested in others. These tasks are easier for someone who is capable of extending oneself and able to engage in open communication.

A.R.T.ful Leaders who are Trusted consistently cultivate interpersonal relationships. The positive impression built by leaders who work at developing interpersonal relationships builds positive trust and often leads to individuals aspiring to emulate this kind of leadership. The ability to create leadership intimacy is a profound influencer and creates a powerful impact on organizational members.

Referent Power Aligned with A.R.T.ful Leadership

Referent Power is demonstrated through the following A.R.T.ful Leadership Drivers and Attributes:

REFERENT POWER DRIVERS AND ATTRIBUTES

ELEMENT	DRIVER	ATTRIBUTES
Admire	Social Dexterity	7 > Networking
	Authentic	8 > Confidence 9 > Connections 10 > Compatibility
Respect	Demonstrate Mutual Respect	18 > Respectful 19 > Approachable 20 > Genuine Interest in Others
Trust	Builds Relationships	37 > Cultivate Interpersonal Relationships

A.R.T.ful Leadership Reflection Journal

1. When Attributes do you possess that reflect Referent Power?

2. Which Attributes do you need to improve in order to leverage Referent Power more effectively?

Coercive power

Coercive Power is power that utilizes force or threats to influence organizational members to comply with a leader's directives. Organizational members are motivated out of fear to take action when subjected to coercion. Coercion is simply the lowest form of motivation, and leaders who use coercion lack the ability to influence organizational members in a more positive manner. Their use of coercive tactics to get organizational members to do what they want reveals their A.R.T.less leadership style.

Forms of coercive power used by A.R.T.less leaders may include threatening a demotion, threatening a loss of pay or a reduction in pay, withholding or passing someone over for a promotion, relocating an individual to an unpopular location, giving someone an unpopular assignment, withholding or diminishing a bonus, and threatening a job loss. It is hard to fathom "leaders" believing that the use of coercive power is an effective way to motivate or have a positive impact on the organization or themselves. Using coercion is merely proof that the leader is unable to lead in any other manner and has no business leading people.

"Leading by Threats"
A Story of Coercion Via Threats

My former leader "Brenda" led by the use of threats. I can say I look back on that time with a tremendous amount of disgust. I consider Brenda's behavior abusive. Thank goodness, I am a tremendously strong individual. She brought others on the staff to tears, which to me is unconscionable. I can only say that it is unbelievable that she is a leader in the organization. Because of her and others like her the organization is an unhealthy place to work.

If Brenda wanted to make a change to the organization, she would roll it out always by email, never in a meeting. Brenda lacked any communication skills. She would threaten to limit information, do things to the structure of our jobs, and threaten to take away responsibilities. Many threats did come true without warning.

One tactic she would use was threatening not to approve our expense reports if we didn't do certain things. Since I traveled extensively I would have thousands of dollars in travel expenses at any given time. So, not approving expenses in a timely manner was a major issue. When she would use this threat I would step forward and remind her that she had to approve valid expense reports because not to do so was against company policy. That made Brenda really mad. It was always a battle and would often have to be escalated, which made things worse in the long run.

Another one of Brenda's veiled threats was to put one of my peers on a bogus performance plan. This was clearly a step to let us know that we better watch it, or we all would be next. It did work; it showed us all that we should be next out the door and away from her. Which is what we did.

It is my experience that the use of Coercive Power within an organization tends to be a systemic problem. When there is a coercive abuse of power there is a very strong likelihood that the organization's culture lacks a clear vision with regard to integrity. The organization does not fundamentally value organizational members.

Organizations that have the following core elements will do well in preventing leaders from having to resort to Coercion as a form of influence within their organizations.

- **Establish an A.R.T.ful organizational culture.** A positive organization culture clearly establishes expectations of how leaders and organizational members are to behave. Organizations that are passionate about establishing positive cultures and holding people accountable will prevent coercive behaviors from being acceptable. To do this successfully at MinuteClinic we built a strategy to infuse A.R.T.ful behaviors into the organization. We built A.R.T. into new employee orientation, manager and leadership training, and organizational culture training. We set expectations and held leaders **accountable** for A.R.T.ful behaviors by building A.R.T. into the performance management system. We also highlighted A.R.T. in our recruiting efforts. Finally, to keep focus and attention on A.R.T., we communicated constantly.

- **Establish clear roles and responsibilities.** Leaders who have established clear roles and responsibilities set clear expectations for performance. Roles and responsibilities provide leaders with a framework to manage performance without resorting to coercion to influence team members. Role clarity provides an opportunity for leaders to positively guide and influence organizational members and provides a context to recognize contributions, determine rewards, and provide ongoing, meaningful feedback. None of these are part of a leader's vocabulary when using Coercive Power.

- **Develop leadership skills.** Organizations must educate leaders on positive techniques to use in influencing and motivating team members. Without this as a requirement leaders may not have the competency needed to do it appropriately on their own. Bad behavior breeds bad behavior.

Coercive Power and Impact on A.R.T.

Coercive Power is the most aggressive and destructive form of power that a leader can use when attempting to influence organizational members. It is also clear that when a leader chooses to use Coercive Power it will have a severe impact on how they are perceived as a leader. Individuals at the core deserve to be treated with respect and dignity, but being subjected to coercion doesn't do either.

It should be fairly evident that the use of coercion negatively impacts a leader being perceived as an A.R.T.ful Leader, one who is Admired, Respect and Trusted. Simply, it is impossible. Coercive Power completely destroys a leader's credibility. Coercion is not effective and is based not on leadership strength but on weakness. The goal of A.R.T.ful Leadership is for a leader to create and sustain true and committed followership. Coercion does the opposite.

Coercive Power Aligned with A.R.T.ful Leadership

Since there is no correlation between A.R.T.ful Leadership and Coercive Power, A.R.T. Drivers and Attributes don't apply. The research is clear that leaders who use Coercive Power are not perceived A.R.T.fully.

A.R.T.ful Leadership Reflection Journal

1. When have you been the target of Coercive Power? What was the situation, and what impact did it have on you?

2. When have you used Coercive Power, and what was the impact on your ability to be perceived as an A.R.T.ful Leader? How could you have done things differently?

3. Which of the power bases do you tend to leverage the most and why? Do you overuse?

4. Which of the power bases do you tend to not leverage and could leverage to increase your effectiveness moving forward to impact your ability to be perceived A.R.T.fully?

The PATH to
A.R.T.ful Leadership

If you are already a leader—one who leads a company, a function, or a department—you have already attained some measure of success. And for that you should be proud. However, being named a leader is only the first step; in and of itself it doesn't necessarily equate to having the ability to *create and sustain true and committed followership*. I believe that the ultimate litmus test of a leader is not how successful you are at climbing the corporate ladder or the amount of money that you have amassed for yourself, the company, and shareholders. All are important, but HOW you lead and influence is even more important.

As a leader you have an amazing opportunity to impact the lives of the people you have been entrusted to lead. As you have witnessed through the countless examples in previous chapters, that is not happening often enough. It is your responsibility and obligation to lead A.R.T.fully in order to maximize your own potential as well as the potential of those you lead and influence.

Being a leader in the general sense is not enough *to create and sustain true followership*; it simply isn't. A.R.T.ful Leaders are leaders who attain a different standard of leadership. They are leaders who through intentionality attain true and committed followership. This creates impassioned performance and enables true synergy within the organization. That is what separates a "leader" from an A.R.T.ful Leader.

A.R.T.ful Leadership requires a leader to be Admired, Respected, and Trusted by those you lead and influence. The success you have as a leader today may not necessarily require this level of achievement, although I am a strong advocate that it should. The rewards that A.R.T.ful Leadership brings to you as a leader, to individuals you lead and influence, to the organization, and to your life outside the organization are tremendous.

The PATH to A.R.T.ful Leadership

This final chapter lays out a step-by-step process that I am calling the PATH to A.R.T.ful Leadership. As you journey down this PATH, you will have the opportunity to learn the process to attain A.R.T.ful Leadership in every facet of your life. The PATH requires diligence and commitment. In the final analysis, it isn't any less work than any other worthwhile endeavor you have set your mind to accomplish. The PATH will require you to look at how you lead from the perspective of the people that you lead and suspend your own perception or ego in the process. So be prepared; this may be difficult, but is essential if you are going to succeed. It will challenge you to respond to how others see you rather than to how you see yourself. This can be difficult, but it is a tremendous growth opportunity.

The PATH will also push you to face some of your vulnerabilities. When this happens you may want to give up; this is natural. After all, it can be easier to keep doing what we are doing rather than to change, even if what we are doing isn't working. Therefore, I recommend that you not walk the PATH alone. Seek someone you A.R.T. to walk the PATH with you. This can be incredibly helpful to stay the course.

The first iteration of The PATH to A.R.T.ful Leadership was introduced at an OptumHealth Leadership Summit. Leaders within OptumHealth were familiar with the research I was conducting outside of my role with UnitedHealth Group and were interested in bringing A.R.T.ful Leadership to their leadership group. The session challenged leaders to begin their own PATH to A.R.T.ful Leadership. You are about to embark on the same challenge.

The PATH to A.R.T.ful Leadership is built around the two foundational questions of A.R.T.ful Leadership:

Who do you A.R.T.?
And
Who A.R.T.s you?

The PATH is a process that will ensure that you understand how you are perceived by those you lead and influence. The PATH provides you with a means to identify where opportunities exist to lead more A.R.T.fully. The PATH provides a process to be perceived as Admired, Respected, and Trusted by individuals who are critical to your success as a leader. The process outlined in this chapter provides the framework for you to be successful in your own PATH to A.R.T.ful Leadership.

As you read this chapter, be prepared to do personal work. Have your journal ready. It may be helpful to read the chapter twice. Read the chapter first without journaling. This will allow you to understand the PATH to A.R.T.ful Leadership. Next, begin the process by completing all the necessary steps from the beginning. Doing this will make The PATH easier to complete. But the most important thing is that you begin the journey. Whatever approach you choose, make sure to take this opportunity seriously and do the work outlined.

> **Note:** The A.R.T.ful Leadership Workbook provides worksheets specifically designed to guide you through each journaling activity. The workbook is available at www.art-fulleadership.com

The PATH: Four Key Steps

The PATH to A.R.T.ful Leadership includes four key steps. Within each "process step," you find questions for reflection and exercises to complete. The process steps on the PATH are:

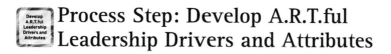 Process Step: Develop A.R.T.ful Leadership Drivers and Attributes

1: Conduct an A.R.T.ful Leadership Assessment

You will begin the PATH by reviewing the A.R.T.ful Leadership Drivers and Attributes found in Chapters 4-6 and in the Appendix of this book. As you assess yourself against the A.R.T.ful Leadership Drivers and Attributes, it is important that you assess your strengths and opportunities through the perspective of those you lead and influence. Begin by identifying which A.R.T.ful

Leadership Drivers and Attributes are strength areas. Next, identify the Drivers and Attributes which you need to strengthen. Make a list of strengths and areas where improvement is warranted to be perceived as an A.R.T.ful Leader.

Note: Assessing your A.R.T.ful Leadership capability can more accurately be accomplished by completing an A.R.T.ful LeadView Self-Assessment or by engaging in the A.R.T.ful LeaderView 360 process. These assessments are designed to measure your abilities against the A.R.T.ful Leadership behaviors that comprise the A.R.T.ful Leadership Model. The assessments are available at www.art-fulleadership.com.

The following questions will help you to accurately identify which Drivers and Attributes are strengths and which are opportunities to develop:

- How am I perceived in demonstrating this Driver/Attribute?
- Do I consistently demonstrate this Attribute as I interface with those I lead and influence? If the answer is "yes," it is a strength; if the answer is "no," it is an opportunity to strengthen.
- Where am I perceived as having gaps by the greatest number of people I lead or influence, which hinders me being perceived as an A.R.T.ful Leader?
- Which of the Attributes would my biggest detractors (or individuals who may not A.R.T. me) say are my biggest opportunities to strengthen?

A.R.T.ful Leadership Reflection Journal

1. Make a list of A.R.T.ful Leadership Attributes that are STRENGTHS. These are the Attributes that you consistently demonstrate.

2. Make a list of A.R.T.ful Leadership Attributes that are OPPORTUNITIES for you to improve in order to be perceived as an A.R.T.ful Leader.

2: Target Attributes to Develop

Development should be extremely focused. If everything is important, then nothing is important. Therefore, be extremely selective in the Attributes that you select to develop. Limit development to no more than three Attributes at a time. Limiting development allows you to balance your continued demands as a leader, as well as focus on strengthening A.R.T.ful Leadership capabilities.

Review the list of Attributes that you have identified as needing improvement. Focus your development attention based on the following criteria:

- Select the Attributes that present the largest gap areas in your PATH to be perceived as an A.R.T.ful Leader.
- Select the Attributes that will result in the biggest perception change once you begin to demonstrate them consistently.
- Select the Attributes that you are willing to commit your time, attention, and effort in developing (in the next three to six months).

A.R.T.ful Leadership Reflection Journal

1. Write down the three (or less) A.R.T.ful Attributes you have identified based on the selection criteria above.

2. Reflect on these Attributes and why you have chosen them. In what ways do they provide the biggest opportunities for you? How are these likely to change the perception others have of your leadership?

3: Develop a Plan

Once you have made your selections it is time to develop an action plan to ensure that you begin developing immediately. As a leader it is likely that you have either been asked to create development plans, or you have instructed others to do so. Although well intentioned, many development processes fall short in actually facilitating development.

Developing a plan requires you to be deliberate. Without a plan you will not be successful. You need to focus on the Attributes you identified above and consider how you can get from point A to point B. Your development PATH may be short or perhaps it may be quite long, depending on the learning curve required for you to demonstrate a selected Attribute consistently. That is what your plan helps you determine.

Long ago during my early days in consulting I had an evaluation I would use after each meeting with a client. I evaluated myself against a set of consulting behaviors that I had devised. After several meetings I realized that I had a listening problem. I was talking way too much and not listening enough. Upon analyzing this, I realized this was most prevalent when I was meeting with new clients. It appeared that I would get nervous and when nervous I would become excessively talkative. I had the KNOWLEDGE of what it took to be a good listener, but I was unable to exhibit the behavior consistently. What I needed to figure out was how to demonstrate what I already knew.

My plan? Write on the top of my notebook (and this is true) the words "SHUT UP" in big bold letters as a reminder to listen more.

In retrospect I could have used a code word, but being part Irish I needed to be direct with myself. I just had to be careful that my clients did not see the words I had written on the top of my notebook during meetings. This trick coupled with my continuous post-meeting self evaluation worked. I became an excellent listener during client meetings in a very short time. To this day when I enter an executive's office for a meeting a small voice in my head says, "Shut Up."

Consider the following elements as you build your plan of action:

- Treat development planning as you do any other planning you do in business.
- Determine whether you need to develop knowledge associated with the targeted A.R.T.ful Attributes. If so, what specific knowledge do you need? How are you going to acquire that knowledge?
- Identify whether you will need to develop skills associated with the A.R.T.ful Attributes you are targeting. If so, what skills do you need to develop? Be specific. How and/or where will you acquire the skills needed to be perceived as A.R.T.ful in the targeted Attributes?
- List the steps you will take to develop the skill.
- List who will be involved in completing each step.
- Put a target completion date for each step. Be realistic in your target dates. The target dates will help you track your progress.
- The most important consideration in developing A.R.T.ful Attributes is to select a Development Coach. This individual is someone who will guide and counsel you through your development. This individual should be someone you perceive as A.R.T.ful and someone who you believe possesses the A.R.T.ful Attribute that you are targeting. Select an individual who knows you well. This will aid you in receiving ongoing feedback needed to progress. Your coach will also direct, instruct, and provide advice—all critical for you to quickly gain competence as expeditiously as possible. Make sure that you ask for their involvement in the process and their commitment as your coach. With your coach, set expectations for the number of times you will meet and how long each meeting will be.

- Identify how you are going to know when you are progressing or improving in the target area. It is critical that you measure progress. How will you know when you are being perceived as A.R.T.ful in this targeted area? This may require you to gather feedback from those you lead and influence.

A.R.T.ful Leadership Reflection Journal

As you prepare to create a plan, reflect on the following questions:

1. Do I need a different plan for each Attribute I am targeting? If so, how will I approach each plan?
2. What knowledge and/or skills do I need to develop in order to address the Attributes I have targeted?
3. How will I gain the knowledge and/or skill I need?
4. What is a reasonable timeline for my development plan?
5. How will I know when I have mastered the A.R.T.ful Attribute I am targeting? Write down some possible evaluation strategies.
6. Who can coach me in my development? Does he or she display the positive Attributes that I am targeting for myself?
7. How will I track and evaluate progress?

4: Take Action

The following suggestions will help you keep motivated and focused as you work your development plan:

- Manage development like all other business requirements. Schedule time to focus on your development, assess your progress, and plan for future progress. Planning is essential for success.
- Ask for help when you face a challenge that you are finding difficult to overcome.
- Determine discrete activities to move forward in your development (work your plan).
- Review progress weekly. If you haven't accomplished what you have intended to accomplish, don't be discouraged. Get back on track.

- Meet regularly with someone who has your best interest in mind (your development coach). Ask for feedback and encouragement. Discuss your progress, challenges, and continued opportunities.
- Continuously seek ways to demonstrate the Attributes you are targeting in daily interactions with individuals you lead and influence. Be particularly aware of those who you believe have perceived you as lacking selected Attributes previously. Remember, lead intentionally.

A.R.T.ful Leadership Reflection Journal

Reflect on the progress you are making by asking yourself the following questions:

1. What have I learned by focusing my attention on this area?

2. What have been the biggest challenges I have faced to date? How can I overcome the challenges to move forward?

3. What have I learned about myself in growing into an A.R.T.ful Leader?

4. What support do I need and/or feedback do I need to determine if I am being perceived more A.R.T.fully in this area?

5. Where have I demonstrated the A.R.T.ful Leadership Attribute, and what was the result?

 # Process Step: Understand How Others View You as a Leader

Leaders who are purposeful in being perceived as A.R.T.ful are aware of how others perceive them. Understanding how others perceive you needs to be done without any pretense. You will need to check your ego at the door. You must be completely open to understanding how others see you and why (seek to understand), without becoming defensive, finger-pointing, rationalizing, or making excuses. As you begin to learn how others see or perceive you, there will be times when how you see yourself is in conflict with how others see you. When we receive information from others that conflicts with our own self-image it can be ego bruising. The likely response is to become defensive in order to protect our self-image.

Consider the following excerpts:

> " . . . I was shocked when I was stabbed in the back by my team. After all I have done for them. They couldn't wait to throw me under the bus."

> "I don't care what Bill has to say. He doesn't respect me, and I don't respect him!"

I have heard comments like these many times over the years as leaders struggle with the difference between self-perception and how they are perceived by others. Responses like these hinder our ability to lead effectively. Reactions like these become barriers to leading A.R.T.fully. But it is clear that until we can accept the perceptions of others, we can't begin to do things differently to change perceptions for the better.

What does this mean for you? It requires that you take a journey of self-awareness and make bold steps to extend yourself and determine how your intentions are being received. Through this understanding you can then become more adaptive, grow as a leader, and lead intentionally. This will help you align how you perceive yourself with how others perceive you. This will result in your ability to lead and influence effectively and become an A.R.T.ful Leader.

1: Prepare for Feedback

How you view feedback is fundamental to your ability to achieve A.R.T.ful Leadership (refer to Chapter 5). A.R.T.ful Leaders are self-aware and seek continuous feedback as a means to understand how they are being perceived by those they lead and influence. It is through feedback that leaders gain understanding of what is working and where opportunities exist to strengthen their A.R.T.ful Leadership.

When seeking feedback you should ask critical questions that will help you understand how you are perceived by others. Phrase questions in a manner that will allow individuals to respond honestly and openly without putting them on the spot. Consider how the following questions are constructed:

- **How am I being viewed as a leader?**
  Phrasing the question in general terms allows individuals to answer more honestly without fear of reprisal or hurting your feelings. Although they may be answering the question in a general context, they are answering it through their personal lens, or how they perceive you to

be. If this question was asked more directly: "How do YOU view me as a leader?" those who are asked would likely be much more edited and cautious with their response.

- **How do people describe my leadership style?**
  Again, phrasing the question without using "you" allows for a more honest answer, but still provides valuable, direct feedback.

- **On a scale of 1 being Not Effective as a Leader and 5 being Highly Effective as a leader, how would the organization rate me and why?**
  Using "organization" rather than "you" allows for a more direct and open answer to this question.

- **How would individuals finish this statement: I lead by . . .**
  Using "individuals" rather than "you" once again provides an opportunity for a more direct response.

Questions can be phrased more directly if you A.R.T. the person from whom you are seeking feedback, and you know that they A.R.T. you. In this case, seeking feedback can become a very candid conversation.

Before seeking feedback from others, answer the questions you are going to ask others yourself. And when you answer the questions yourself, be brutally honest. Doing this allows you to analyze your self-perception against how others perceive you as a leader.

A.R.T.ful Leadership Reflection Journal

1. In addition to the questions above, make a list of up to 10 specific questions for which you would like to receive very specific feedback. Ask questions concerning specific responsibilities that you have as a leader. Reflect on each question and answer the questions for yourself as honestly as possible.

2: Seek Feedback

Varied and rich feedback is what will make you a more A.R.T.ful Leader in the eyes of a wide audience. Seek feedback from enough individuals to make it relevant. Tap a variety of perspectives within the organization (and outside the organization if it makes sense). Don't just relay on individuals who you know are your strongest advocates.

Follow these simple guidelines to ensure you are receiving relevant feedback:

- When possible, select individuals you A.R.T. When you select individuals you Admire, Respect, and Trust you will be more likely to heed and pay attention to their feedback, no matter how harsh it may appear.
- Seek feedback from five or six of the key individuals that you must influence as a leader.
- Have the courage to seek feedback from individuals that may not A.R.T. you. It is important to gain their perspective in order to determine how to be more effective in leading and influencing them moving forward. Remember, all feedback is valuable (see Chapter 5).
- Consider seeking feedback from individuals both inside and outside the organization.
- Add a couple of individuals who are part of your social network; this provides an additional perspective.
- Schedule a time with each individual to gather feedback. Just don't send a meeting invite via email. It is very important to invite people verbally (in person, if possible) to provide you feedback. When you do, tell them you have selected them to provide you feedback because you *value their perspective*. If you A.R.T. them, say it! This opens lines of communication and encourages them to honestly answer the questions you have of them.

A.R.T.ful Leadership Reflection Journal

1. List individuals that you LEAD and/or INFLUENCE as part of your leadership role. Select individuals whose feedback you think would be of most value. In addition, select two individuals from your social network to gather feedback. Make sure you have at least THREE individuals providing you feedback for each of your questions. If you don't, determine if you can ask another individual the question, or determine if you can expand your list of feedback candidates.

2. Review the list and determine which names on the list you A.R.T. and which names on the list A.R.T. you.

3. Review each question you have developed. It is important to ask relevant questions to the right people. You will not ask the same questions of everyone on your list. Select individuals that you believe will provide the best feedback for each question.

4. Arrange the list of people above in the order you want to interview them and solicit their feedback

3: Look in the Mirror

After you have gathered feedback, really take time and discover what you have learned. This requires you to Look in the Mirror and carefully consider each piece of feedback that you have collected. This can be difficult depending on how ego-involved you are and what feedback people have shared.

When you receive feedback that is less then complementary, you need to resist becoming defensive and instead take a moment and consider what you can learn from the feedback. This is the only PATH to achieve A.R.T.ful Leadership. Ask yourself the following as you consider each piece of information you have collected:
- What is my contribution to this perception?
- What is my obligation to change moving forward?

Answering these two questions honestly is truly owning feedback and being responsible and accountable, which are two Attributes of an A.R.T.ful Leader. In addition, consider the following while evaluating the feedback you have collected:
- How do I see myself?
- How do others see me?
- Where are the gaps?

The answers to these questions will set your course from where you currently are to where you want to be, and how you intend to get there.

I ask these questions to leaders individually during coaching sessions and in groups. I also pose these questions to people I know in my private life as I challenge them to look in the mirror. This may be why I don't have many friends (I do hope you chuckled). I also wrestle with these questions continuously myself (just ask my wife how many times I explain a situation I am in and then ask, "Am I wrong?" I won't tell you her answer). They can be extremely challenging depending on certain situations and people involved. But the answers are important to becoming a better leader and person in my community and my home. The revelations and insight that this process brings is the conduit for making positive changes moving forward.

A.R.T.ful Leadership Reflection Journal

Answer the following questions as a means to reflect on who you are as a leader and to consider the feedback you have received and what you have learned from the feedback.

Questions to reflect on your leadership in general:

1. What are key life-lessons that have contributed to who you are?

2. If you could tell someone three things that you are most proud of, what would they be and why? How do these impact how you lead? If they don't currently have an impact, how could they make a positive impact on how you lead?

3. What are your greatest achievements as a LEADER and why?

4. What brings you TRUE joy? Is there enough of this joy in your life? Why or why not? If there is not enough joy in your life, what can you do about it, and how could this impact your leadership?

Questions to reflect on the feedback you received:

1. After each interview, write notes about what you heard. How is this process helping you?

2. From the feedback you received, what was most gratifying?

3. What surprised you from the feedback you received? What hurt you?

4. What feedback was hard to listen to or accept? Why?

5. What gaps exist between how you see yourself as a leader and how others see you as a leader?

6. What barriers do you need to overcome to be more effective moving forward?

7. Where are you most confident?

8. Where is your greatest opportunity to increase your A.R.T.ful Leadership capability moving forward and where are you committed to take action?

9. Based on the feedback and your own reflection, answer the following: Where are you currently at as a leader? Where do you want to be? How do you intend to get there (the answer to this is to continue on the PATH)?

Process Step: Conduct a Relationship Review

Being an A.R.T.ful Leader is an intentional act and requires you to be cognizant of who A.R.T.s you inside and outside the organization.

A.R.T.ful Leadership is based on creating mutually beneficial relationships in which you as a leader A.R.T. those you lead and influence, and they in turn A.R.T. you. Therefore, it is important for you to identify the critical relationships you have as a leader and to assess those relationships to determine how A.R.T.ful each of them is in relation to your ability to lead and influence effectively. Without knowing who A.R.T.s you, your chance of being viewed as an A.R.T.ful Leader will fall short. That is what this step in the PATH of A.R.T.ful Leadership is all about.

Some of this work has already been done if you have sought feedback from the right individuals, asked the right questions, and gathered information that provides insights regarding your ability to create and sustain positive relationships. Along with this information, you need to review the relationship status of individuals you lead and influence in order to identify where opportunities exist to strengthen relationships with key individuals.

When you are seeking opportunities to improve relationships, you need to be reflective and rational. This process requires you to once again check your ego at the door and be as analytical as possible. This is a non-emotional exercise. If you struggle with this, you will not be able to take responsibility for why you are perceived the way you are by certain individuals. A.R.T.ful Leaders have the foresight to do this without pretense. Consider the following conversation that illustrates how a leader may struggle with coming to terms with a relationship review:

Larry: So let's discuss John. Why is it that your relationship with him is challenging?

Peter: Because he has been out to get me since I joined the organization.

Larry: What specifically is it that is causing a relationship strain between you and John?

Peter: Everything! He tries everything he can to make my life difficult.

Larry: Give me an example of what John does that makes it difficult for you to work with him effectively.

Peter: Only one? I can give you a hundred!

(Peter starts talking, but doesn't provide specific examples; he merely provides a long list of grievances about what John does that annoys Peter. As he talks he becomes more and more agitated. I wait and let him talk. When he is finished, I let us both sit in silence for about 20 seconds, which seems like an eternity to Peter. I do this to let Peter think about what has just happened. How Peter has responded. As the seconds tick by I sense the Peter realizes what he has done.)

Larry: Peter, what I am recommending is that we look at your relationship with John as an opportunity. An opportunity that when improved, will allow you to be more effective as a leader. What I sense is that you are frustrated by the current situation with John. I appreciate that. At the same time you realize that you are required to work with John's organization. This constant tension tends to magnify your frustration. Is that an accurate summary?

Peter: Yes.

Larry: So it would make sense to look at things differently and identify ways to improve the relationship in order to reduce your frustration and allow you to be more effective. Does that resonate with you?

Peter: That is why his name is top on the list.

Larry: So let's keep that frame of reference as we move forward and look at ways that are in your control to move things in a positive direction. Agreed?

Peter: Agreed.

A relationship review requires you to complete the following steps:

1: Identify Individuals Critical to Your Success

Make a list of people inside and outside the organization *who are critical for your success as a leader.* These include individuals who are above you, beside you, and people that you lead and influence. When reviewing relationships, be selective at first. You can always expand the list. Many of the individuals may be the same people you sought feedback from earlier in the process. Be thoughtful in constructing the list. This isn't about promote-ability or politics; it is about leadership effectiveness.

2: Determine the Relationship Status

Classify each name on the list of relationships in the following ways:
- **Relationships are "strong"** when you A.R.T. the individual and you believe the individual A.R.T.s you.
- **Relationships "need strengthening"** when you do not A.R.T. an individual or you believe an individual does not A.R.T. you. You will focus on improving these relationships moving forward to increase your A.R.T.ful Leadership effectiveness.

3. Identify Barriers

Identify the barriers that exist for each of the relationships that you have identified as "Need Strengthening."

When you do not A.R.T an individual, you will typically perceive that the individual does not A.R.T. you as well. Remember, A.R.T.ful relationships tend to be reciprocal. Therefore, it is important that you identify the barriers that exist which are causing relationship strain. To identify barriers:

- **Look in the Mirror.** I know you are getting really tired of Looking in the Mirror, but as you do this it gets easier, and you will gain self-awareness. Take the viewpoint of "How can I be more effective with this individual moving forward?" rather than one of "What have I done wrong?" The former is positive and forward thinking; the latter is negative and backward thinking.
- **Define three to four barriers for each relationship that needs strengthening.** Clearly describe the barriers that are standing in the way of a reciprocal A.R.T.ful Relationship.

  Answer the following questions for each individual on the list:

  What are the barriers that exist for me to be more effective in creating an A.R.T.ful relationship?

  What is standing in the way of truly having an open and honest dialogue and connection with this individual?

- **Determine** what *you* may be doing to contribute to the relationship strain. What could you be doing differently to improve the relationship? It may be helpful to review the A.R.T.ful Leadership Drivers and Attributes during this process. What A.R.T.ful Leadership Attributes might you need to exhibit more of when relating to a particular individual to improve the relationship? The answer to this may provide you with insight on how to begin to make progress.

- If necessary, ask someone who knows both of you to provide a perspective that you may not think of on your own.
- Use the feedback you gathered whenever possible as a source to identify barriers. If you did not receive feedback from key individuals you may choose to pause and seek feedback before continuing the PATH.

4: Devise Strategies

Many times individuals will ask me, "Why should I have to take the first step?" or "Why do I have to change when I am not the one that is making things difficult?" It is simple; only you have the power to change your own behavior. You can't force someone to change their behavior or actions. However, when you change how you interact, this changes the dynamics of the relationship. This causes a fundamental shift or response from the other person.

It is *your* obligation to take the first step to move a relationship in a more positive direction. After all, you have identified the relationships that are critical to your success as a leader. In the final analysis it really is all about you. It is YOU taking the necessary actions needed to lessen resistance from key individuals who are critical to your success in increasing your leadership effectiveness. It may appear that you are giving in, but it really is about being intentional in your actions—to lead A.R.T.fully.

Devise strategies to remove each of the barriers that you have identified. Strategies should be specific behaviors or actions that you control, that you believe are realistic, and that will evoke a positive response. Identify two actions per barrier to prepare yourself to make progress. Write strategies or actions as "I will . . ." statements. You will begin to deploy these actions or behaviors the next time you have an opportunity to interact with each of the individuals you have targeted.

A.R.T.ful Leadership Reflection Journal

1. Before you prepare to conduct a relationship assessment, spend a few moments reflecting on why you are taking this step on the PATH. What will happen if you don't take this step in the process? How do think things will change if you don't?

2. Complete the following steps to help you assess relationships that are key to your success.
   - Make a list of the individuals that you believe are critical to your leadership success.

- Look closely at each individual you have identified on the list. For individuals that you believe A.R.T. you and you A.R.T. them, categorize this relationship as "Positive." For individuals that either don't A.R.T. you or you don't A.R.T. them, categorize this relationship as "Need Strengthening.
- Identify Barriers that exist in the relationships that you have identified as "Need Strengthening." Write down three or four specific barriers that exist between you and the individual. Be as specific as possible. What is lacking? What communication barriers exist between the two of you? What happens when you and the individual interact? What do other individuals say and do, which cause problems between you and those individuals? Guard against making a list of grievances.
- Devise strategies. For example, identify two actions you can take (that you directly control) to help break down each of the barriers you have identified. Write actions as "I will . . ." statements.

Process Step: Strengthen Relationships

Once you have identified relationships that need to be strengthened and have created specific actions to remove barriers, it is time to take action. This will require you to make a concerted effort to reestablish and reengage individuals you have targeted as critical to your success. The following steps will enable you to engage each individual in a new and more positive relationship. This will result in widening your ability to be perceived as an A.R.T.ful Leader.

1: Have a Fresh Start Conversation

Initiate a Fresh Start Conversation. This crucial first step is key to your success in building relationships based on A.R.T. Depending on the situation, this may be quite difficult. The more strained a particular relationship is, the more difficult or uncomfortable it will be for you to initiate this conversation. If you are hesitant, it is an indication that a particular relationship is severely strained and is in dire need of strengthening. So buck up and as Nike would say: Just Do It!

> **Note:** An exercise I conduct during coaching sessions is to have executives complete a "readiness score" for each relationship that needs strengthening. I do this exercise so that executives are clear about how motivated they are to actually take the necessary actions to strengthen relationships. For each individual relationship the executive rates how willing they are to move forward. A rating of 1 indicates that they are "unwilling and hesitant" to

move forward; a rating of 5 indicates that they are "ready and anxious" to move forward to strengthen the relationship. We then discuss the "1" and "2" ratings to bring clarity to why they are hesitant and to remove resistance. We discuss the importance of moving forward with the most strained relationships. You may find this exercise helpful in your own PATH to A.R.T.ful Leadership.

Request a meeting: Contact each individual and request a meeting. As before, request the meeting orally (either in person or on the phone) before sending a meeting invite. Position the meeting to discuss ways to "work more effectively" or "work more collaboratively." Refrain from discussing specifics or any problem areas (barriers) that exist between you and the individual. If pressed, merely state that you have been thinking about opportunities to be more effective and look forward to discussing these with the individual. Keep it positive.

During the Meeting: During the meeting you will, in essence, verbally walk through the Relationship Review you conducted. Begin by stating your intentions to create a more positive relationship with the individual. Your intentions can be determined by answering the following:

- What caused you to request this discussion?
- Why is a more collaborative relationship important to you?
- Why is a more collaborative relationship important to the other individual? What is in it for them?
- What barriers exist (from your perspective)? Make sure to position barriers in a way that doesn't place blame on what the individual is doing wrong, but on what could be done differently going forward. Also frame it in relation to what you can control.
- What do you want to see happen in the future?
- What can the person expect to see you do differently to improve the relationship? These are from the "I will" statements you have prepared.
- What do you need from the person you are meeting with to ensure that the relationship improves going forward?

Approach each meeting in a conversational manner. Use "I" and "We" language as much as possible. Avoid using "you" terms that will likely put the individual you are meeting with on the defensive. *Relationships often become stuck when individuals continuously rehash why things haven't worked and communicate backwards instead of focus on communicating forward.*

Therefore, it is important that you focus on what positive changes can be expected moving forward to improve the relationship. Learn from the past, but focus your attention on the future. Finally, keep this as brief and focused as you can. Be realistic about how much can be achieved in moving the relationship forward; after all, Rome wasn't built in a day. Strengthening relationships will take time.

2: Take Action

Once you have had a Fresh Start Conversation, be deliberate and intentional about doing things differently. Utilize the strategies that you have devised to improve each relationship and follow through on each discussion. At first it may be difficult and awkward as you re-pattern your behavior and learn a new way to interact. Acknowledge these moments when they occur; maintain an open and honest dialogue about what you are intending to do. Communication is critical. This is why Communication is a Driver that impacts all three elements of the A.R.T.ful Leadership Model. As you begin to create new patterns of behavior with individuals and learn new ways to engage more positively, relationships will begin to strengthen. This is an incremental process. With diligence and focus your efforts will be rewarded.

3: Continuously Assess Your Progress

Assess each interaction in order to determine if the strategies and actions you have implemented are actually working. Determine if your intentions are being met with positive responses. If not, determine what adjustments need to be made to achieve positive progress. You can assess progress by answering the following:

- Overall, how would I rate the interaction (1 = poor / 5 = excellent)? Why do I give the interaction this score?
- Did I follow my intentions?
- What went well during the interaction?
- Did my intentions match my behaviors during this interaction? If not, what do I need to do differently next time?
- What did I find awkward during the interaction and why? How can I improve this next time?
- What didn't work? Why?
- What do I need to discuss with this individual to keep things progressing forward to improve the relationship?
- Continuously assess: Do I A.R.T. this individual? Does this individual A.R.T. me?

You will notice that the above questions are all "I" related. Why? Once again, this is because only you can control your own behavior.

As you lead by positively changing how **you** interact with others it will begin to influence how **they** interact with you. When appropriate, share the list of questions above with individuals you are working with. Express how helpful you have found these questions to be in making positive relationship progress. You may also suggest that they use the questions as an aid to make positive progress in working more effectively together. Better yet, evaluate progress together. This will truly create a genuine partnership that will accelerate the strengthening process.

4: Discuss Progress

Once you have deliberately and consistently changed how you have interacted with the individual overtime, AND have recognized consistent improvements, it is time to have an open an honest discussion concerning the progress you both have made. This is an opportunity to acknowledge the impact that improving the relationship has had on each of you as leaders, and how it has impacted your team, your organization, and the business. In addition, discuss the opportunities and challenges that still lie ahead to continue to strengthen the relationship. Discuss the work that you both need to focus on to keep things moving forward. Position the continued work as "possibilities" rather than as "threats" to the relationship. The key is to keep the discussion positive and hopeful that the investment you have made has proven successful and is worth continued focus.

The following questions can be used to discuss progress:
- What has been going well during interactions that has increased our effectiveness in working more positively together?
- Wheat specific things have I noticed in the past (weeks/months) that have been encouraging in working with you?
- What is different?
- What is going better? What has improved?
- How is the progress we have made impacting me, the organization, and the business?
- How can we ensure that we stay on track?
- What is one thing that would lead to a more effective relationship? Answer this question with an "If we . . ." statement.

Strengthening relationships take time. There is no magic bullet. It will require time, attention, and focus by both parties. It will also require you to lead the effort. Depending on the severity of the problems that exist in your relationships, you may need to seek help from a relationship coach, communication coach, or executive coach who can be a tremendous help in improving your ability to master interpersonal relationships. In addition, such support can be used to practice conversations that may be difficult for you to initiate at first.

A.R.T.ful Leadership Reflection Journal

1. Think about the critical relationships that aren't working today. What if you just kept doing the same thing tomorrow that you are doing today? Would things change without considering committing to this action? What are your biggest fears as you consider taking concrete steps to strengthen your working relationships? What are your hopes for this step in the process?

2. Conduct a Fresh Start Conversation with individuals that you have identified as Need Strengthening. You will find it easier to begin conversations with individuals where the least strain exists and the fewest barriers exist . Starting with these conversations will help you build confidence to tackle the more difficult relationships and conversations.

3. Remember, strengthen all relationships that are critical to your success as a leader. This is about your leadership effectiveness and your ability to be perceived as an A.R.T.ful Leader. By taking action and setting the example, you can fundamentally change how you are perceived and your ability to make positive impact. This is an incredible opportunity.

4. As you work to strengthen each relationship, continuously assess incremental improvements.

5. Discuss the overall improvements with each individual when consistent progress has been made as a means to acknowledge relationship success.

6. Always, always ask: Who do I A.R.T.? AND Who A.R.T.s me?

"The Transformation"
A Story of Investing in a Relationship

The transformation that occurs when one invests in strengthening a relationship on both a professional and personal level is quite extraordinary. Time and time again I hear how beneficial following the PATH is to leaders and how the PATH has enriched their lives both professionally and personally. The PATH is a process of self-growth and relationship growth and can be tremendously rewarding as the following illustrates.

As a consultant, relationships are critical to my success. Matter of fact, I pride myself in my ability to connect with people. Not this time. When I was beginning my assignment with a particular executive, things became very difficult for me. It was clear from the start that he was not interested in establishing a relationship. In fact, it seemed he would likely not desire to form a relationship with anyone. He was not communicative, was incredibly critical, and "partnering" was simply not in his vocabulary. This was going to be hard. As I began to try to work with him he was unable (or perhaps he simply refused) to articulate what he really wanted. In retrospect I don't think maybe he knew what he wanted and therefore his internal frustration was manifested negatively. It was clear from the start that he had severe control issues and trust issues.

Every time we met he drilled me about every little detail. I felt like a punching bag. He was relentless and criticized everything. Nothing was ever good enough, nothing was quite right, but when asked to provide feedback to clarify he was unable to. Instead he would create barrier after barrier to progress.

I had an impeccable track record within the organization, which is why I had been referred to this individual and this assignment. However, I was stumped why he had requested to work with me, since he made it nearly impossible to be successful. I had never stepped out of an assignment before, ever, but I was close to it for the first time. But before I did, I decided it was time to stop pointing fingers at him and conduct a relationship review before throwing in the towel.

I used my network within the organization to seek feedback and determine how to best approach this leader. I was very careful not to appear as though I was complaining about him, in case my conversations got back to him. Everything that I was able to gather supported what I was experiencing; the guy was brutal, harsh, indecisive, and argumentative. What a reputation he had built for himself. I also learned that I had been selected because of my ability to work with difficult individuals (information that I was not told initially going into the assignment). Somehow this information didn't make me feel better. No one seemed to know how to make it work with this guy. In fact, the best advice I received was to "buck up and take it like a man!"

I concluded that what I was experiencing was not different than what others in the organization experienced in working with this individual. Though this information helped me feel better personally, it did nothing to help me figure out how to be more successful. So now, what?

I had to take a hard look in the mirror and try and figure out how to approach the executive differently. As I considered how I could evoke a different response from the executive I had an idea. He scrubbed every detail and picked apart every nuance. I, on the other hand, had been approaching our meetings with a more relational and conversational approach. I had been using a high-level agenda and provided verbal updates, for the most part. I would

193

provide details that I had either in files or on my computer as needed. This approach had been extremely successful in the many consulting engagements that I had within the organization in the past. However, it dawned on me that this approach was likely driving him crazy, because he wasn't a relationship guy, lacked trust, was highly analytical and demanded control. Based on this, I realized what I needed to do differently was to evoke a different response. It was worth a try, because the current path I was on was contributing to the A.R.T.less relationship. So I decided to change it up and see what happened.

At the next meeting, rather than providing him a high level overview, I apologized (yep, I sucked it up) for not being diligent enough in providing details that he may have desired, and that I wanted to change things moving forward. This approach, I believed, would help us to have an opportunity to effectively partner. The report I handed him was highly structured and was bound. It included a table of contents, included statistics, tables, graphics, current detailed status, and clear descriptions of what would be coming next (what I would be doing and what he would be accountable for providing). In past assignments this level of detail would not be needed, since others in the organization would have access to the details and the executive would be given only the snapshots (an Executive Summary so to speak). So, this was a clear departure from what I had provided him in the past.

I aggressively drove the meeting—no small talk, no trying "relationship-talk," no conversational language—just business. Surprisingly, he didn't push back and didn't respond negatively to any of the information. As I took him through the report at a very aggressive pace he had to concentrate to keep up with me (I did this intentionally). As I went through the report I would make sure he understood the information, but I didn't ask him if he had any questions (because I knew if he did he wouldn't hesitate to speak up). He was attentive and was focused on the report. I had never seen him so engaged. He asked few questions, and when he did they were relevant and clarifying; none were negative or accusatory.

At the end of the meeting I asked him what he thought of the new report format. In typical fashion, he was critical; he thought the report was too long. I told him that I would see what I could do to trim the report a bit but that he should expect the same format because clearly we were on the right track. He agreed.

From that meeting forward I kept this format with very minor changes. And progress started to be made. As a result, meetings took less time because he started to gain confidence in me. After several weeks he started to request meetings to be canceled (which I didn't allow because face time was essential). Over time he would quickly review the report himself instead of me walking him through the report. Then he would want to take the rest of the time together to discuss other organizational issues with me and get my advice. Trust was beginning to form.

Over time he began to actually have conversations with me—actual conversations that added depth to our partnership—yes, partnership. We began to form a relationship, and he began to ask me for advice on leadership issues on a personal level. As the relationship continued to strengthen it was evident that he valued my opinion. His behavior had changed dramatically. What I realized is that it was me who had to initiate the change, and it was me who had to interact with him differently for a more positive relationship to form. It is very strange indeed, but our relationship changed so dramatically that I actually considered him a friend. We have even discussed our remarkable transformation several times and have admitted how frustrating we found each other to be at first. We have stayed connected over the years; sometimes we connect for business reasons and other times merely to connect as friends. The PATH truly is worth the investment.

The PATH to A.R.T.ful Leadership increases your ability to lead intentionally, strengthens key relationships, and helps you be perceived as an A.R.T.ful Leader. As you follow the PATH you will benefit yourself and those whom you engage in the process. You will find that following the PATH to A.R.T.ful Leadership will become easier each time. You will become more aware of how others see you. You will master the ability to assess relationships. You will gain agility in adapting your approach to strengthening key relationships. And you will become intentional in leading A.R.T.fully. Through your ability to lead intentionally you will begin to influence others towards their own PATH to A.R.T.ful Leadership.

It may be slow at first, and you may be met with resistance by some. Some simply will not want to participate or desire to strengthen a relationship with you. Why? Simply put, they are A.R.T.less leaders. The reasons are many and are contained in previous chapters. Do not let these A.R.T.less individuals destroy your own PATH to A.R.T.ful Leadership. Don't let them have that power. Why should you? Instead, focus your attention on the vast majority of individuals who will desire a relationship that will be mutually beneficial. These individuals understand that they will increase their own effectiveness by working with you. Those are the relationships that are well worth the investment.

The PATH to A.R.T.ful Leadership is a process that requires self-analysis, relationship analysis, interpersonal self-awareness, and the ability to lead intentionally. At times this process will stretch you and take you to places that are not comfortable for you. These moments will test your ability to truly be A.R.T.ful in how you respond to challenges. You will have the opportunity to do things differently or ignore the opportunities and continue to struggle.

The benefits to you both professionally and personally will be great when you choose the Path to A.R.T.ful Leadership. Taking the Path is your choice alone.

The goal of A.R.T.ful Leadership is to create true followership and sustained commitment from those you lead and influence. The PATH to A.R.T.ful Leadership is the process that will allow you to reach that goal.

Visit www.art-fulleadership.com for additional tools and resources to aid you on your PATH to A.R.T.ful Leadership.

A.R.T.ful Leadership: Change your leadership, and impact your team, your organization, and your life.

"The Essence of A.R.T.ful Leadership"

Once again complete the following activity that you first completed before beginning reading the book. This will be a gauge in how far you have come in your own Path to A.R.T.ful Leadership.

1. Access the following link and watch the 2-minute video:
   http://www.art-fulleadership.com/what-is-art/

2. Answer the following questions:
   - What are your reactions to the video?
   - Were you able to answer the questions?
   - Which ones couldn't you answer, and why?
   - What would it mean to you, your team, or you organization if you were able to answer the questions with confidence?

A.R.T.ful LEADERSHIP DRIVERS AND ATTRIBUTES

ELEMENT		DRIVER	ATTRIBUTES
SKILLED COMMUNICATOR	**ADMIRE**	Deliver Consistent Results	1 > Strategy 2 > Operational Plan 3 > Execute Flawlessly
		Competent	4 > Knowledgeable 5 > Leadership Ability 6 > Tenacious Drive to Succeed
		Social Dexterity	7 > Networking
		Authentic	8 > Confidence 9 > Connections 10 > Compatibility
		Represents with Credibility	11 > High Moral Compass 12 > Values 13 > Integrity 14 > Reputation
	RESPECT	Supportive	15 > Loyal 16 > Dependable 17 > Encouraging
		Demonstrate Mutual Respect	18 > Respectful 19 > Approachable 20 > Genuine Interest in Others
		Responsible and Accountable	21 > Responsible for Own Actions 22 > Sets Expectations 23 > Holds People Accountable
		Provides Feedback and Counsel	24 > Seeks Feedback 25 > Provides Feedback
		Fair and Balanced	26 > Provides Opportunities to All 27 > Rewards and Recognizes 28 > Consistently Resolves Issues Fairly
	TRUST	Extends Trust	29 > Vulnerability 30 > Sharing Information 31 > Building Confidence 32 > Sharing Power
		Keeps Confidences	33 > Maintain Confidentiality 34 > Courage to be Candid
		Honest	35 > Clear Standards 36 > Speak the Truth
		Relationship Builder	37 > Cultivate Interpersonal Relationships
		Collaborative	38 > Leverage Talent 39 > Seek Input

Notes

Chapter 1

1. Nordhagen, Larry R. *A.R.T.ful Leadership Characteristics Survey* (Minneapolis: Pinnacle Performance Systems, Inc., January 2009, March 2009).

Chapter 3

1. The term "Soup Nazi" was made famous by an episode of the TV show *Seinfeld*.

Chapter 4

1. Maxwell, John C. *The 21 Indispensable Qualities of a Leader* (Nashville: Thomas Nelson, 1999) p. 81.

2. http://sportsbusinessdigest.com/penn-state-merchandise-sales-down-40-since-scandal/ Emmett Jones/November 22, 2011.

Chapter 5

1. Blanchard, Ken and Johnson, Spencer. *The One Minute Manager* (New York: HarperCollins, 2003), p. 39.

2. Giving and Receiving Feedback Effectively, Pinnacle Performance Systems Inc. 2003. Minneapolis, MN.

3. Giving and Receiving Feedback Effectively, Pinnacle Performance Systems Inc. 2003. Minneapolis, MN.

Chapter 6

1. Zand, Dale E. *The Leadership Triad* (Oxford and New York: Oxford University Press, 1996).

2. Looking Out Looking In; Ronald B. Adler, Neil Towne; Pages 288-292; Holt, Rinehart and Winston, Inc. Sixth Edition; 1990

   Dyadic Communication; William W. Wilmot; 3rd Edition; pg. 183-190; Random House, New York; 1986

   Leading A.R.T.ful Teams; Larry R. Nordhagen; 2011; Pinnacle Performance Systems, Inc.

3. Adler, Ronald, B. and Elmhorst, Jeanne Marquardt. *Communicating at Work* (New York: McGraw Hill, 2008), pp. 139-143.

4. Nordhagen, Larry R. *A.R.T.ful Leadership and High Performing Teams* (Minneapolis 2006: Pinnacle Performance Systems Inc., 2006).

Chapter 7

1. The *A.R.T.ful Leader View 360 Assessment* measures how leaders are perceived by key individuals inside and outside the organization. This carefully crafted assessment measures A.R.T.ful Leadership effectiveness against the 16 A.R.T.ful Leadership Drivers. The assessment provides an A.R.T.ful Leadership Quotient for each of the three elements of A.R.T.ful Leadership and assesses a leader's ability at achieving organizational balance. Based on direct feedback, the *A.R.T.ful LeaderView 360* provides leaders with powerful feedback needed to truly realize A.R.T.ful Leadership. Pinnacle Performance Systems Inc. provides *A.R.T.ful LeaderView 360* assessment solutions to individual leaders and teams. Information can be found by visiting www.art-fulleadership.com.

Chapter 8

1. Raven, B.H. and French, J.R.P. Jr. "A Formal Theory of Social Power," *Psychological Review*, Vol. 63, 1956, pp. 181-194.

ABOUT THE AUTHOR

Larry R. Nordhagen is the founder and president of Pinnacle Performance Systems Inc., a firm dedicated to providing A.R.T.ful Leadership tools and resources to assist today's leaders and prepare tomorrow's leaders to create and sustain true followership and commitment from those they lead and influence. Larry is known as an expert in organizational design and development and leadership. He formed Pinnacle Performance in 2002 and consulted on a wide-range of organizational issues to increase effectiveness from leadership, change management, sales and cultural transformation.

In 2006 Larry was approached to lead the learning organization for MinuteClinic, which at the time was making plans to expand nationally. Although it was a difficult decision to leave his practice, the opportunity to once again create a learning organization and be part of the origins of the retail healthcare movement was a compelling proposition. After his departure from MinuteClinic, Larry joined UnitedHealth Group as the Director of Learning and Development and Strategic Consulting before returning to Pinnacle Performance to lead the A.R.T.ful Leadership consulting practice.

His ability to connect with individuals, whether during a keynote address or during a leadership session makes him truly impactful. Through storytelling Larry relates A.R.T.ful Leadership to real-life lessons. In addition, his openness allows others to be open.

Larry's educational background includes an undergraduate degree in Communications and Management from Concordia College and a Masters Degree from the University of Montana and North Dakota State University. He holds many assessment certifications he uses in executive coaching in addition to authoring the A.R.T.ful LeaderView 360 assessment. He has studied at the University of Michigan executive center and the Mager Institute.

About A.R.T.ful Leadership Solutions

Pinnacle Performance provides a comprehensive arrary of solutions aimed at improving A.R.T.ful Leadership capability in leaders and organizations. Through executive coaching, consulting and training we partner with organizations to ensure leaders achieve breakthrough results by leading A.R.T.fully.

Coaching and Assessments
- A.R.T.ful Leadership Executive Coaching
- A.R.T.ful LeaderView 360
- A.R.T.ful LeaderView Self-Assessment

Leadership Training
- Leading A.R.T.ful Change
- A.R.T.ful Leadership POV
- 10 Rules to A.R.T.ful Leadership
- The Path to A.R.T.ful Leadership

Consulting
- A.R.T.ful Cultural Transformation

Certification
- A.R.T.ful LeaderView Certification

Pinnacle Performance Systems, Inc.
8678 Boiling Springs Lane
Minneapolis, MN 55379
WEB:www.art-fulleadership.com
EMAIL: info@art-fulleadership.com
PHONE: 612-237-9230

Index